Buster Keaton's "Sherlock Jr." focuses on a classic by one of America's greatest silent film geniuses, whose films still delight and amaze audiences worldwide. The essays included here, written especially for this edition, examine this film in the context of Keaton's career, and offer new perspectives, among other things, on its unusual production history, Keaton's vaudeville background, and the differing views of "masculinity" that both celebrate and poke fun at cinema itself. Also included is a filmography of Keaton's works, contemporary reviews of *Sherlock Jr.*, and a select bibliography.

Buster Keaton's *Sherlock Jr.*

CAMBRIDGE FILM HANDBOOK SERIES

General Editor

Andrew Horton, *Loyola University, New Orleans*

Each CAMBRIDGE FILM HANDBOOK contains essays by leading film scholars and critics that focus on a single film from a variety of theoretical, critical, and contextual perspectives. This "prism" approach is designed to give students and general readers valuable background and insight into the cinematic, artistic, cultural, and sociopolitical importance of selected films. It is also intended to help readers better grasp the nature of critical and theoretical discourse on cinema as an art form, a visual medium, and a cultural product. Filmographies and select bibliographies are included to aid readers in their own exploration of the film under consideration.

Buster Keaton's
Sherlock Jr.

Edited by

ANDREW HORTON
Loyola University, New Orleans

CAMBRIDGE
UNIVERSITY PRESS

PUBLISHED BY THE PRESS SYNDICATE OF THE UNIVERSITY OF CAMBRIDGE
The Pitt Building, Trumpington Street, Cambridge CB2 1RP, United Kingdom

CAMBRIDGE UNIVERSITY PRESS
The Edinburgh Building, Cambridge CB2 2RU, United Kingdom
40 West 20th Street, New York, NY 10011-4211, USA
10 Stamford Road, Oakleigh, Melbourne 3166, Australia

First published 1997

Printed in the United States of America

Typeset in Stone Serif

Library of Congress Cataloging-in-Publication Data

Buster Keaton's *Sherlock Jr.* / edited by Andrew Horton.
p.   cm. – (Cambridge film handbook series)
Filmography: p.
Includes bibliographical references and index.
ISBN 0-521-48105-8 (hardcover). – ISBN 0-521-48566-5 (pbk.)
1. Sherlock Jr. 2. Keaton, Buster, 1895–1966. I. Horton,
Andrew.
PN1997.S4717B87   1997
791.43'028'092 – dc21   96-50387
                                                          CIP

A catalog record for this book is available from
the British Library.

ISBN 0-521-48105-8
ISBN 0-521-48566-5

Contents

Contributors

Dan Georgakas is a founding editor of *Cineaste* and the author of several books, including *The Methusla Factors* (Simon & Schuster, 1980), *Cineaste Interviews* (Lakeview Press, 1988), and *In Focus: A Guide to Using Films* (Zoetrope Press, 1979). He teaches film and media courses at New York University and Cornell.

Michael Goodwin was an editor of *TAKE ONE* film magazine and is the author of many film articles and reviews for the *Village Voice, American Film, Premiere, Playboy,* and other journals, as well as the book (with Naomi Wise) *On the Edge: The Life and Times of Francis Coppola* (New York: Morrow, 1989). He is currently working on a book about carnival in Trinidad and a book about New Orleans street culture.

Andrew Horton is Editor of the Cambridge Film Handbook Series and the author of numerous film studies, including *Comedy/Cinema/Theory* (editor, University of California Press, 1991), *Inside Soviet Film Satire: Laughter with a Lash* (Cambridge University Press, 1993), *The Films of George Roy Hill* (Columbia University Press, 1985), and *Writing the Character-Centered Screenplay* (University of California Press, 1994). He is Professor of Film and Literature at Loyola University, New Orleans.

Henry Jenkins is Director of Film and Media Studies at Massachusetts Institute of Technology. His books include *Classical Hollywood Comedy* (editor, with Kristine Brunovska Karnick, Routledge, 1995) and *What Made Pistachio Nuts? Early Sound Comedy and the Vaudeville Aesthetic* (Columbia University Press, 1992).

Kathleen Rowe Karlyn teaches film studies at the University of Oregon. She has published articles in the *Quarterly Review of Film Studies*, the *Journal of Film and Video*, *Jump Cut*, and *Screen*. Her book, *The Unruly Woman: Gender and the Genres of Laughter* (University of Texas Press, 1994), is a study of the outrageousness of women in film and television comedy.

Peter F. Parshall is a Professor in the Department of Humanities, Social and Life Sciences at Rose–Hulman Institute of Technology (Terre Haute, Indiana). He has published widely in journals including *Literature & Film Quarterly*, *Film Criticism*, and the *Journal of Film and Video* and teaches courses in American film comedy and Japanese cinema.

David B. Pearson is Managing Editor of the *Driftwood* newspaper at the University of New Orleans and has built up an impressive silent comedy collection, reflecting his strong interest in Keaton and other silent comedians.

Acknowledgments

This collection and, indeed, the Cambridge Film Handbook Series would not have come about without the guiding vision, intelligence, and good humor of Beatrice Rehl, the Fine Arts and Media Studies Editor at Cambridge University Press. Mary Racine deserves special thanks as one of the finest production and copy editors I have known. That she also watched *Sherlock Jr.* enough times not only to appreciate Keaton's genius, but to catch many of us in this collection on errors of memory of the film, says much about Mary's dedication to the volume. Finally a hearty thanks to my wife, Odette, and children, Sam and Caroline, who have laughed with me many evenings as we have viewed and re-viewed Keaton's timeless comedies.

Buster Keaton's *Sherlock Jr.*

ANDREW HORTON

Introduction

"THINK SLOW, ACT FAST" –
KEATON'S COMIC GENIUS

> We smile not *at* Keaton, but at *ourselves,* and
> it is a smile of health and Olympian strength.
>> (Luis Buñuel)

BUSTER KEATON ENDURES

Cinema and Buster Keaton both celebrated their hundredth birthday in 1995. Such longevity not only suggests the durability of cinema as a mass medium and Keaton as one of its foremost comic filmmakers, but also reminds us that many films and filmmakers have not survived. This collection of new essays is a celebration and a critical analysis of Keaton's enduring comic genius for a contemporary audience. Our focus is on one of his most memorable films, *Sherlock Jr.* (1924), the comic tale of a young movie theater projectionist who has two loves: his girl and his desire to be a detective.

It is fortuitous that the completion of this book coincides with the release of many of Keaton's nineteen two-reelers and ten feature comedies on video and laser disc (see the Filmography). For it is now possible once again to experience silent comedy in much of its original glory. In fact, before turning to an introduction of our contributors and their essays, I wish to start with an undergraduate student's reaction to a January 1995 New Orleans screening of *Sherlock Jr.* from a released video copy, presented in an auditorium with jazz pianist Tom McDermott playing live to Keaton on the screen. Like most of the others in this standing-room-only crowd, this student was encountering Keaton for the first time, and this was certainly his first experience of hearing live music playing to a silent film. The student writes of this encounter: "I was captivated not only by Buster Keaton and his amazing physical acting, but by the techniques used to make the film. I was shocked to see some of these techniques in the film because I had no idea that they had been around so long – for instance, the dream sequence when Keaton leaves his own body to explore his fantasy, and also when he steps into the movie screen to enter a separate reality. The piano accompaniment to the film made me feel as if I were in an audience in 1924 seeing the film for the first time. And just the look of Keaton's stone face left me asking a hundred questions. I always thought that silent comedy was just slapstick comedy, but Keaton proved me wrong with his expressionless face." This student's reactions were similar to many others expressed that evening, and so this volume is dedicated to helping a new generation understand the captivation that audiences of Keaton's day experienced.

Keaton remains, quite simply, one of the most innovative American screen comedians – especially in silent comedy. He managed to combine his vaudeville roots with a strong grasp of the medium of film itself, and through mime and acrobatic comic gags, he developed unsentimental and ironic narratives that spoofed conventional American stereotypes and beliefs. We have selected *Sherlock Jr.* from among his splendid features both because it is still such a delight to watch and because it clearly illustrates the crossroads of several traditions of American film and stage comedy, mime, satire, and parody that Keaton embodies. *Sherlock Jr.* is particularly appropriate for those interested in the development of film as a medium because so much of the comedy is generated out of a playful and ironic bending of the conventions and dimensions of cinema as it had evolved to that time.

Let us turn to the film itself to provide a background for the discussion to follow on Keaton's comic talent and the place of that talent in the tradition of American screen comedy and, indeed, in the tradition of comedy itself.

SHERLOCK JR.: A SYNOPSIS

Sherlock Jr. is a silent comedy feature built around Keaton's efforts as a small-town cinema projectionist to win the love of his "girl" (Kathryn McGuire); after his rejection by her on trumped-up charges initiated by a rival suitor, it becomes a film-within-a-film as Keaton dreams he enters the movie he is projecting to become Sherlock Jr., investigating and solving a crime that leads to his winning the love of the girl he thinks he

FIGURE I
Buster courts "the girl" (Kathryn McGuire) at her home. *Sherlock Jr.* (Courtesy of the Academy of Motion Picture Arts and Sciences, Los Angeles.)

has been denied in real life. It is, in fact, as we shall discuss further, both a parody of many of the typical melodramas of the day and, as Kathleen Rowe Karlyn establishes, a comic take on the popularity of Sherlock Holmes.

The film breaks neatly into five segments. The first takes place at the small-town cinema where Buster, "the boy," is employed. The second involves his courtship of "the girl" and subsequent problems with a rival suitor, "the sheik," and the third is concerned with Keaton returning to the cinema to project a film but falling asleep and having his dream double attempt to enter the movie being projected. The fourth segment is the film-within-the-film, which, because it is actually a dream of a film, becomes cast with those that Keaton is involved with: his girlfriend, the sheik, and the girl's father, among others. The final segment concerns the concluding romance as Keaton awakens to find the girl in the projection booth with him, having discovered Keaton's innocence of the crime he was accused of.

Segment 1

At the film's opening, Buster Keaton is seated in an empty movie theater reading a book on how to be a detective. The cinema owner comes in and angrily points to a pile of rubbish Buster has not swept up. We now realize Buster's position: he is a cinema janitor and, as we shall discover, a projectionist to boot. When he starts sweeping up outside the cinema, he discovers a few dollar bills, but loses them to various characters who come by claiming they have lost money. Undaunted, Keaton goes to a nearby sweetshop and purchases a dollar box of chocolates but changes the 1 on the price tag to a 4 as he heads for his girlfriend's home.

Segment 2

It is clear that he hopes to become engaged to the girl (she is, in the tradition of the times, never identified as more than "the girl"), for he gives her the chocolates, turning over the box to make sure that she sees the $4 on the bottom, and then a ring. But the stone is quite small, so he hands her a magnifying glass to see it better. Their courtship doesn't get far before the sheik (a common name for the villain in silent films) arrives and causes a multitude of troubles. He has brought an even bigger box of chocolates after pawning the girl's father's watch, which he has stolen. Furthermore, the sheik places the pawn ticket for the watch in Keaton's pocket and then conveniently "discovers" it there when the watch is declared missing and everyone is searched. Keaton, in disgrace as a suitor and as a would-be Sherlock, is told to leave the house and never return.

Then follows a hilarious routine as Keaton tries to trail the sheik, but does not succeed in cracking the case.

Segment 3

Meanwhile Keaton returns to the cinema and cranks up the projector for the film of the day, a melodrama entitled *Hearts and Pearls*. As he falls asleep next to the projector, his ghostlike dream self climbs out of his sleeping body, looks through the projection booth window, and watches the characters on the screen become transformed into those he knows: the girl, the sheik, and the girl's family.

The dream-Keaton walks down into the audience and up to the screen and jumps into the movie. The screen is set up like a live theater production, and he is booted out of the "screen" and back into the pit. When he jumps again, he lands inside the film, and thus begins a comic sequence in which he becomes the victim of film language as the landscape changes, seemingly at random, forcing Keaton to dive, jump, fall, dodge, and climb, all in reaction to seas, railroads, mountains, lions, and so on. Finally, however, the dream-Keaton is integrated into *Hearts and Pearls,* and the film-within-the-film begins.

Segment 4

In this "projected" dream, Keaton is no longer a victimized young cinema janitor and projectionist, but rather Sherlock Jr., complete with a tuxedo and top hat, and the cinema

FIGURE 2

Buster studies his book, *How to Be a Detective,* in his girlfriend's home, surrounded by (left to right) the hired hand (Erwin Connelly), the girl's father (Keaton's own father, Joe Keaton), the girl's mother (Jane Connelly), the girl (Kathryn McGuire), and the sheik (Ward Crane). *Sherlock Jr.* (Courtesy of the Academy of Motion Picture Arts and Sciences, Los Angeles.)

owner himself is transformed into Sherlock Jr.'s "sharp" assistant, Gillette. A string of pearls has been stolen from the girl's home, and Sherlock Jr. has been called in to recover them. Meanwhile the sheik and his partner are trying every means possible to destroy Sherlock, by setting up poisoned drinks, dangerously wired seats, and an explosive 13 ball on the pool table. But Keaton manages to outwit them all and to pocket the 13 ball bomb, substituting a real ball.

The search becomes a chase as the sheik and Sherlock leave the mansion, opening what looks like a safe, which leads to the street outside. The most elaborate gags take place as Keaton with the assistance of Gillette attempts to retrieve both the pearls and the girl, who has been whisked away to a secret hideout. There are chases, including the famous one in which Keaton rides the handlebars of a driverless motorcycle (Gillette has been knocked off the cycle without Keaton's noticing) and a sequence in which Keaton retrieves the pearls and dives through a window and a hoop resting in the window frame which contains a dress, thus allowing Keaton in one swift move to escape and emerge as an old woman walking off to the complete – if only temporary – confusion of the criminals.

Finally Keaton saves the girl from a fate worse than death (the possibility of rape), and the two escape in a car as Keaton blows the pursuing criminals away with the deadly billiard ball. Alas, Keaton's car is hurled into a lake and, as it begins to sink, he and his girl appear to be drowning instead of driving off happily into the sunset.

Segment 5

Keaton awakens from his dream in the projection booth to find that the girl has arrived to tell him she has solved the crime committed by the sheik in framing Keaton. She is clearly fond of the boy, but he is unsure of how to act in such circumstances until he glances through the projection booth window at the movie playing on the screen. Imitating the action onscreen, Keaton gives a ring and a kiss to his appreciative love. But then Keaton is stumped. His last glance at the screen reveals the male lead bouncing twins on his knees. We see Keaton scratch his head as "The End" appears.

KEATON: THE FACE, THE GLANCE, AND THE ACROBATIC BODY

Keaton's face is not as expressionless as the student suggests above. It is, rather, *unsmiling* (Keaton says he learned very

FIGURE 3
Buster Keaton in 1922: the deadpan gaze, even offscreen. (Courtesy of KINO Video, New York.)

early in his vaudeville career that he got more laughs if he did not smile), giving the impression that he is reflecting on something in his mind. "Think slow, act fast," Keaton writes in his autobiography with reference to his way of doing comedy. And it is certainly true that one of the basic elements of Keaton's comic genius is the tension between his fast and agile actions (one critic compared his body to a "coiled spring") and his motionless, inward-reflecting gaze. In *Sherlock Jr.*, for instance, there are numerous occasions in which these elements – the slow thinking and fast action – are played against each other. Often, Keaton simply lowers his head, thoughtfully, for an instant before he acts, as in the early scene outside the movie theater when he finds a dollar in the trash and a woman stops by to claim it. The brief nod is enough to suggest the inner struggle – he wants the money to buy a box of chocolates for his girl, but the woman apparently has a valid claim – which is resolved with a swift action as he hands her the dollar. But the face and the slow thinking can involve a longer take than this, as memorably captured in the closing scene of the film. As several of our contributors have noted, Keaton is standing by the projection booth window, looking at the big screen in the auditorium for clues as to how to act with his girlfriend. He has already kissed her and placed a ring on her finger. But in one simple cut the next scene on the screen shows the hero bouncing twins on his knees. Keaton remains framed by the projection booth window scratching his head. This time there is no action! And we are left to puzzle too. Is the Keaton figure too innocent to know how to make babies or is he suddenly aware, as Kathleen Rowe Karlyn suggests in her essay, that romance may lead him where he does not wish to go? Either way, it is Keaton's face, and its thoughtful, deadpan, puzzled expression, that we are left with. "Keaton's face is a riddle considerably more difficult to unravel than that of the Sphinx," comments French critic Jean-Pierre Lebel.[1]

Keaton began making his own two-reelers by 1920, and already in 1921 critics were beginning to tag him the "Great Stone Face." Of course silent comedy, as we shall discuss further, celebrates comic actions, including all the slapstick physical actions that involve every part of the body. Keaton certainly had the body of a trained acrobat, and was able to do incredible stunts by himself without a double. But it is important that as early as 1921 it was his unsmiling face, his sad-eyed glance, his elegant youth, and his vulnerable expression that became something of a trademark for critics and audiences alike. "The camera likes him," Robert Benayoun explains in his book devoted to, as the title announces, *The Look of Buster Keaton*.[2]

Keaton's gaze was unique. Chaplin's face – those sad eyes,

that child-man look of both cunning and curiosity – was also memorable. And other silent comics had their trademarks. But as the first century of cinema ends, we keep returning to . . . that face. Clearly this would not be the case if Keaton's face did not speak to us on some level that we perhaps do not completely understand but that we nonetheless find appealing. The early film star Louise Brooks, who was a good friend of Keaton's, expressed this fascination well: "Since childhood I have thought Buster Keaton's the most beautiful face of any man I have ever seen."[3]

But we should not forget the importance of Keaton's slim body and his physical skills. Keaton makes his stunts look easy. In *Sherlock Jr.* think of his many falls, his leap through the hoop as he escapes from the criminals, his unforgettable ride on the handlebars of the driverless motorcycle, and his shadowing of the sheik through an intricate dance of movements. A comparison with any contemporary comedian reminds us how rare an acrobatic talent Keaton was. Currently, for instance, Jim Carrey has captured the Hollywood comic spotlight, but there is certainly nothing in *The Mask* or *Dumb and Dumber* or *Batman Forever* that comes close to the physical brilliance of Keaton's performances. So much of what we laugh at in *The Mask* has more to do with computer-animated special effects (the heart bouncing out of Carrey's body, for example) than with Carrey's abilities as a physical performer.

Yet to gain a greater appreciation of Keaton, we should consider him within the larger framework of American film comedy and the comic in general.

KEATON AND THE AMERICAN TRADITION OF FILM COMEDY

Before turning to American film comedy, we should ask ourselves a larger question: what is comedy? The question is too broad to answer in depth in this brief introduction, and I have written about it in more detail in a previous book, *Comedy/*

Cinema/Theory. But some points can be made here that will be useful for our discussion of Keaton and American film comedy.

Overall, we can consider the comic spirit to be a particular *perspective* on life rather than simply a genre of theater, literature, cinema, or speech (jokes or witty sayings, for instance). No event or character or action is inherently comic or tragic. What is considered laughable or sad depends on context, attitude, custom, and tradition. Laughter itself is highly unpredictable. Haven't we all found ourselves laughing at tragic moments, suggesting that laughter can be a protective form of release from pain as well as an expression of pleasure? In fact, no better identification of the often-ambiguous blending of the comic and the very serious can be found than in the final pages of Plato's *Symposium,* in which Socrates and Aristophanes, the great comic poet, agree that comedy and tragedy often have much in common, serving as a cathartic means of purging fears and anxieties and leading to insights about the human condition.

Comedy in the broad sense embraces much more than simply that which is funny. The title of Dante's great poetic Christian vision, *The Divine Comedy,* for instance, suggests that the comic is in some sense a triumph over obstacles, in this case in Dante's quest for God. Furthermore, as Ludwig Wittgenstein, among others, has explained, comedy is an important form of "games" or "play."[4] What helps to characterize comedy as a subset of the playful is some understanding of limits, of boundaries, of "rules," and therefore of distance, so that real fear, for example, does not enter as a danger. A game is, after all, a game only if all the players know the rules. Similarly, the very fact that a film is labeled a comedy is only the beginning of a dialogue between creators, performers, and audience in which a certain field of expectations and limitations is established.

Within this framework, comedy in general, and American film comedy specifically, has tended to fall into two categories. First, beginning with the stage comedies of Aristophanes in ancient Greece, is the tradition of anarchistic comedy. This type of comedy focuses on characters (or a character) who come up with an unusual idea, which after surmounting certain obstacles they succeed in carrying out, thus transforming society. For Aristophanes in such comedies as *Lysistrata, Peace,* and *The Acharnians,* the "wild" idea is to end war. And in each case, through exaggerated actions such as the sex strike to end war in *Lysistrata,* peace is obtained and society is changed in accordance with the main character's wishes. We can call this brand of comedy "anarchistic" because the characters do not do what all of us in real life must do: compromise in order to survive. Such comedy is the most imaginative and fancy free, for it is not necessarily bound by any laws or rules of reality as we know it. In American film, anarchistic comedy is reflected in much of silent comedy, from the Keystone Cops to Laurel and Hardy and many others, and in sound film, from the Marx Brothers and W. C. Fields to John Belushi and more recently Jim Carrey and even Beavis and Butt-head, among others.

Second, a major category of comedy that has developed in Western cultures is romantic comedy. Romantic comedy embraces a variety of styles and modes, but in general it emphasizes not only romance but the need for personal and social compromise in some form so that the couples involved and thus their society may continue. From the Romans to Shakespeare and on to Hollywood with the highly developed screwball romantic comedies of the 1930s and 1940s, including such films as *It Happened One Night, Bringing Up Baby, Palm Beach Story,* and *His Girl Friday,* romantic comedy has been an enduring genre, especially in America. Many of the popular box-office hits of recent years, including *Annie Hall, Pretty Woman, When Harry Met Sally,* and *Something to Talk About,* continue to mix romance and comedy with endings that unite the most disparate of couples, and we can understand that such forms of comedy clearly speak to millions.

Given this very simple division between anarchistic and romantic comedy, part of what makes Keaton so unusual and so much his own man is that he does not fit easily into either category but, rather, straddles both.

In form, *Sherlock Jr.* must be considered a romantic comedy, for the whole narrative is structured around the boy's efforts to gain the affection of his girl. And yet, within this conventional framework, the girl plays almost no role in the development of the jokes, the gags, the humorous twists and turns that make up the film. For it is, in fact, the anarchistic world of Keaton's dream life within his own film that takes over the major portion of the comedy. And within this dream world, Keaton is much more closely aligned with the fantasy triumphs of Aristophanes than with the social romantic comedies of pathos and humor found in Shakespeare and reflected, during Keaton's time, in Chaplin's films, which went for the heart as well as the laugh. No sentimentality is attached to Keaton's "romances" as it is in Chaplin's films. Rather, building on his vaudeville background, Keaton constructed his narratives, as did many early film comedians including Keaton's mentor, Roscoe "Fatty" Arbuckle, around "gags, gags and more gags around a nice little story," as Keaton once explained.[5]

We thus feel that Keaton stands at a unique crossroads in American film comedy, with a nod toward romantic comedy, but marked by an irony that denies sentimentality, and more than a nod toward "gag" comedy. The combination of these two, plus Keaton's unusual face and gaze, which seem to be, as we have already suggested, beyond any of the action taking place, is part of what makes Keaton so memorable.

The well-known Czech novelist Milan Kundera, speaking on the comic in general, is helpful here: "The real geniuses of the comic are not those who make us laugh hardest but those who reveal some unknown realm of the comic. The comic brutally reveals the meaninglessness of everything."[6] I would suggest that the tension between the slow thought (Keaton's face) and his fast actions reveals something of this "unknown realm of the comic."

Finally, we should go beyond Keaton's enduring power to the larger world of American comedy itself. The great French critic André Bazin always claimed that comedy was America's strongest genre. What might it be about American film comedy, silent and sound, that has been so attractive and memorable not only for Americans but also for millions the world over? The easy

FIGURE 4
Buster Keaton with his wife, Eleanor, at the 1962 Berlin Film Festival.

answer is that laughter is a great cure for, or at least escape from, the stress and tensions of everyday life. But from the pie-throwing early silents through Keaton and Chaplin, the Marx Brothers, Jerry Lewis, and Woody Allen and on to Robin Williams in *Mrs. Doubtfire* or to the sheer nuttiness of *Wayne's World* and Jim Carrey's growing body of farcical triumphs, we can see comedy as more than just a movie genre.

As the next section suggests, there is often a strong contrast between a comedian's life onscreen and his background and life offscreen.

FIGURE 5
Buster Keaton, age 7, while part of "The Three Keatons" vaudeville act, c. 1908. (Courtesy of KINO Video, New York.)

KEATON, THE MAN

My story is also the story of my father.

(Buster Keaton)[7]

That comedy by nature suggests a transcending of
adversity becomes apparent when we contrast the humor of
Keaton's films with the often dramatic events of his life. Joseph
Keaton was born on October 4, 1895, in Piqua, Kansas, in a room
rented by his vaudeville acting parents, who were currently on
the road with Dr. Hill's California Concert Company traveling

medicine show. His mother was Myra Edith Cutler (1877–1955) and his father was Joseph Hollie Keaton (1867–1946), who later appeared in many of Buster's films, including *Sherlock Jr.* His godfather, Harry Houdini, at the time another vaudevillian and friend of the family, dubbed the child "Buster" when he saw the way he was thrown around on stage.

Born into theater and constant travel, young Joseph joined his parents' stage act in 1898, which became known as "The Three Keatons" and in which he played a miniature version of his father. He grew up on the road, in boardinghouses, onstage and backstage, soaking up the craft of acrobatic comedy, perfect timing, and the ability to read a particular audience and give it what it wanted in a stretch of time never exceeding sixteen minutes (the length of time vaudeville acts could last). According to Keaton, "The reason managers approved of my being featured was because I was unique, being at that time the only little hell-raising Huck Finn type boy in vaudeville."[8]

Joseph Keaton appreciated Joseph, Jr. "He's a corker," he once wrote Houdini.[9] But the years of wear and tear and the father's growing alcoholism led to the breakup of the family act in 1917. That same year the twenty-one-year-old Buster met Roscoe "Fatty" Arbuckle, who had made a name for himself in Mack Sennett's Keystone films and had recently begun making his own films with producer Joseph M. Schenck. At the time Fatty was shooting *The Butcher Boy* in New York, and invited Buster to be in it. Although his role was small, Keaton became hooked.

Keaton moved to California later that year when Schenck transferred production to Long Beach and Keaton's mother established California as her home. World War I was on, and Buster was drafted in 1918 and sent to France. After the war, Keaton found himself forming a company on a handshake with Schenck while Arbuckle moved on to feature films. Keaton completed nineteen shorts in the next three years before turning to features.

Financial success followed his growing popularity. From $40 a week working with Fatty, Buster was in 1925 making more than $250,000 a year as well as 25 percent of the profits on his films.

In 1921 he married Natalie Talmadge, though the marriage proved difficult from the beginning as she went through money faster than he could make it. They had two sons, James and Robert. If Keaton's onscreen sweethearts are sweet, if clumsy, Natalie, despite Keaton's lifetime love for her, finally made marriage impossible.

Meanwhile Keaton made a memorable series of features, including *The Three Ages* (1923), *Our Hospitality* (1923), *Sherlock Jr.* (1924), *The Navigator* (1924), *Seven Chances* (1925), *Go West* (1925), *Battling Butler* (1926), *The General* (1926/7), *College* (1927), and *Steamboat Bill Jr.* (1928). If Joe Schenck had helped Keaton at first, he turned out to be the downfall of this acrobatic comedian. On Schenck's advice, Keaton gave up his own company and moved to the MGM grounds as a member of the MGM team.

Then in 1933 came his divorce from Natalie in which he lost all: wife, home, money, children, and even the Keaton name once Natalie went to court and succeeded in erasing even that legacy of the children's father. It may have been a sign of the times that Keaton's crack-up occurred at the same time as that of another great American artist who had given Hollywood a try, F. Scott Fitzgerald. That same year Keaton announced he had given up film making and married Mae Scribbens, a sanitarium nurse whom he met when he was suffering from his father's disease, alcoholism (they were divorced in 1935).

Two-reelers were still being made at the time, and in 1935 Keaton returned to the short-format genre, doing work he himself knew was inferior to his earlier films. From 1937 to 1950 he was also on salary at MGM as a gag writer for Red Skelton, the Marx Brothers, Abbott and Costello, and others.

In 1940, when he was forty-four, he married Eleanor Norris, twenty-one, and the relationship lasted till his death. He did some film work and also traveling theater until 1949, when James Agee's essay in *Life* magazine mentioned him, launching his television career and leading to his rediscovery across the world.[10] But just how sad his life on the road had become before

FIGURE 6
Buster clowning with his sons, Robert (left, age 8) and Jimmy (right, age 9). (Courtesy of KINO Video, New York.)

this rediscovery is captured by Walter Kerr in his fine study, *The Silent Clowns:*

> I trailed him to Hoboken, New Jersey, in 1949, where he was appearing in a shabby stock company production of *Three Men on a Horse.* There he was, idly sauntering into an on stage bar to casually throw one leg over it, forgetfully to throw the other over it a minute or two later, and of course take a thumping five-foot fall on his back. . . . I went backstage to chat with him afterward and had rather a long wait. The man who came from the shower was in a state close to total physical exhaustion.[11]

All of that changed, however, in roughly the last decade of his life. In 1950 he had a role in *Sunset Boulevard,* and in 1952 he gave a touching performance with Charlie Chaplin as an aging vaudevillian in Chaplin's *Limelight*. Bit parts followed in a series of films, including *It's a Mad, Mad, Mad, Mad World, A Funny Thing Happened on the Way to the Forum*, several Beach Party movies such as *Beach Blanket Bingo*, and numerous television appearances. But by all indications, the recognition that meant the most to him was the standing ovation he received shortly before his death at the Venice Film Festival in 1965.

He died in 1966 at age seventy of lung cancer.

KEATON AS THE AMERICAN HERO IN REVERSE

Daniel Moews has observed that the Keaton hero is "the reversal of the American ideal: he is a hero through no intention of his own."[12] And yet others have pointed out that in comparison with Charlie Chaplin, the best-known figure in the world when his films were most popular, Keaton appeared very "American." The seeming contradiction is, I offer once again, an indication of the depth and breadth of Keaton's accomplishment. He is a hero in *Sherlock Jr.* through no intention of his own. It is, as Karlyn explains in her essay, the girl who solves the case in "real life," not Sherlock Jr. Furthermore, as Parshall's essay makes clear, it is Gillette, his "sharp" assistant, who saves the day and solves many of the problems created in the film-within-a-film. And it is by chance that he climbs onto the handlebars of a motorcycle and is thrown through the window of the correct cabin so that he can save his girl.

Clearly the most memorable scene in the film in terms of catching Keaton between intention and chance, design and victimization, is the moment when he attempts to enter the film. As he falls from one frame and one scene to another in a random montage of images that is not tied to any narrative other than his dream of a film, we delight in the sheer inventiveness of Keaton playing with the medium long before the endless attempts to do the same in less brilliant exercises such as *Last Action Hero*. Yet our pleasure derives both from the randomness of the cuts and from Keaton's earnest efforts to adjust to each new frame, only to find that what he thinks up becomes inappropriate action in the next context.

Many would rush to label him "postmodern" in his self-conscious presentation of the medium in which he is appearing. Keaton, however, would never have agreed to such a label. If anything, he and we can see his character, as Pearson, Jenkins, and Parshall suggest in their essays, as one caught not only between the frames of one scene and another, but also between his vaudeville past and his cinematic present, between live performance and cinema as a medium that can destroy and alter time and space and preserve the present at the same time.

Add to this that Keaton is "American" to the degree that he is not the Tramp, the outsider, the outcast, the one who, like Chaplin at the end of so many of his films – short and feature length – waddles down a road, his back to the camera, alone. Despite his questioning of himself or American middle-class domesticity, or both, as he scratches his head at the end of *Sherlock Jr.*, the boy is still with his girl while holding down a job . . . in the movies.

"Keaton made you laugh, then think," Rudi Blesh wrote.[13] I would add that after the thinking comes a final smile, the very smile Keaton purposely denied himself onstage and onscreen.

FILM STUDIES AND *SHERLOCK JR.*

Keaton's comedies are unheard chords, harmonies struck in space and time and requiring no other form of amplification.
(Walter Kerr)[14]

"If Keaton is Sherlock Jr., then we (the audience) are Sherlock III as we gradually uncover this irony," David Rodowick writes, capturing both the fun and complexity of the viewer's perspective in watching Keaton's film.[15] The essays in this collection have been commissioned to help you succeed in your role as Sherlock III. As stated in the Cambridge Film Handbook series page, our goal is to offer a variety of perspectives on a particular film text, in this case *Sherlock Jr.*, which you may then apply in your viewing and study of other films and groups of films. In line with the goal, I have selected essays that explore the cultural, artistic, and sociopolitical implications of Keaton's art in general and *Sherlock Jr.* in particular in the context of American film comedy, American culture, and American history, as well as in relation to Keaton's own life and career. It is my hope that in such a context the essays will help you "open up" Keaton's film to further thoughts, investigations, and discussions.

In Chapter 1, Henry Jenkins explores the borders of vaudeville, silent comedy, and Hollywood narrative in *Sherlock Jr.* More particularly, he analyzes four Keaton films, the early shorts *Back Stage* (1919) and *The Play House* (1922), as well as *Sherlock Jr.* and the sound comedy *Speak Easily* (1932), in which Keaton is teamed with Jimmy Durante. In each case Jenkins demonstrates in vivid terms "the tension between the vaudeville aesthetic and the classical Hollywood cinema."

Jenkins details how each of these films facilitates and motivates extended comic sequences that allow Keaton to display the "performance virtuosity characteristic of the vaudeville tradition" expressed specifically through a motif of disrupted performances, a motif, Jenkins points out, that Keaton used throughout his career. This essay reveals how fleeting such a cinematic clown- or star-centered form of comedy was before narrative-centered comedy quickly won out over such vaudevillian modes. Jenkins concludes that, of the four films, *Sherlock Jr.* is the only one that frames its consideration of performance in terms of cinematic rather than theatrical traditions, thus becoming a "meditation on how classical stories are told."

Chapter 2, by Peter Parshall, compliments and builds on Jenkins's study by exploring how one element of Keaton's vaudeville experience – magic – as best represented by his godfather, Houdini, is used in *Sherlock Jr.* "The word 'magic' has a variety of connotations," Parshall writes, "almost all of which are captured by this film." We therefore are asked to consider Keaton in a broader realm of comedy than has traditionally been studied. In this light, Parshall shows us how stage magic, as Keaton knew it from vaudeville, becomes a variety of magical forms in this film, including magical escapes (Houdini's trademark), dream magic (the film-within-a-film), and a more general magical movement "from failure to fantasy triumph." A particularly original insight arises as Parshall details the magical transformation of the cinema owner into Keaton's able assistant, Gillette, in his dreamed film.

Kathleen Rowe Karlyn's essay, in Chapter 3, begins with the ending of *Sherlock Jr.*, in which Keaton, our young protagonist who has now won the love of his girl, scratches his head when twin babies appear on the screen in the film that he has been watching for cues as to how to behave in his own life. "What causes his paralysis before the specter of domestic life with the woman of his dreams?" Karlyn asks, and proceeds to use feminist and the newly emerging masculine studies to help illuminate "the mystery of manhood" in *Sherlock Jr.*

Karlyn's essay draws on Keaton's entire career to suggest that he "often plays an adolescent boy on the brink of adulthood, staring ahead with uncertainty at the prospects of adult heterosexual love." Her investigation leads her to critique the whole Sherlock Holmes parody and to see the figure of the detective himself as an ambiguous "figure of liminality, deriving his power from his contact with the margins and boundaries of our culture." Karlyn makes it clear that in fact it is the girl who solves the crime in "real life" when she discovers that the sheik has framed Keaton. The result is that Keaton winds up playing the centuries-old cathartic role of the Fool.

"The famous image of Keaton balancing on the handlebars of a riderless motorcycle," Michael Goodwin writes in Chapter 4, "perfectly poised in a world of trouble, could be the central metaphor for his entire filmic career." Goodwin points out more clearly than any previous commentator how "mathematical" so many of Keaton's gags were. The result, as Goodwin explains, is not just the audience's laughter and pleasure at Keaton's physical prowess and wit, but also a certain metaphysical satisfaction that goes beyond the usual realm of comedy. As Goodwin observes about the gags constructed around the efforts of Keaton's sleeping self to enter the film in progress, "This amazing sequence reveals a modern, existential vision in which change is constant but underlying principles hold." Finally, Goodwin offers his own take on why our innocent hero scratches his head at the end of the film: Keaton can handle all the math up to this point, but with the sudden appearance of twins on the screen outside the projection booth, our lovestruck projectionist is undone by multiplication!

In Chapter 5 Dan Georgakas suggests the economic and class structure stated in or implied by Keaton's film. As Georgakas notes about the moment when Keaton enters the screen to become part of the movie he is projecting, "The Sherlock Jr. who enters this realm is no longer of the working class. The dreamer's sense of competence, of being 'classy,' indeed of having 'class,' requires a complete rejection of working-class dress, behavior, and taste." Georgakas concludes by noting that Hollywood cinema presents "instructions" for its audiences coded in narratives that "always reflect, directly and indirectly, the dominant culture as defined by its most prosperous classes." He goes one step further in his concise analysis by tying in Keaton's film to Woody Allen's "reverse" homage to *Sherlock Jr.*, *The Purple Rose of Cairo*, in which the filmic character walks off the screen into the "real" world.

Finally, in Chapter 6 David B. Pearson provides a playful and provocative production history of *Sherlock Jr.*, combining evidence and hypothesis, like a true detective, in an attempt to solve several mysteries regarding the film's production. I can think of no one in the United States who knows so many details about Keaton's films and, indeed, about silent comedy, than David Pearson; thus we can take seriously his sleuthing of three important issues: who actually directed *Sherlock Jr.* – Keaton or his longtime friend and mentor, Roscoe "Fatty" Arbuckle? Why is the film only five reels long when most silent comedies, in-

FIGURE 7
Buster Keaton in *The Navigator* (1924).

cluding Keaton's, consisted of either six or seven reels? And, finally, in what order was the film shot and what consequences did such a shooting order have?

KEATON'S LEGACY

Keaton's legacy continues, much more clearly than one might expect. *Entertainment Weekly* paid tribute to Buster Keaton and *Sherlock Jr.* when it did a follow-up to the box-office flop of 1993 *Last Action Hero*. In a piece titled " 'Jr.' Achieve-

FIGURE 8
Buster Keaton portrait shot. (Courtesy of KINO Video, New York.)

ment," this popular American magazine noted, *"Last Action Hero*'s big gimmick – mingling the worlds of the movies and reality – may seem wildly high-tech, but it's actually as old as hand-cranked cameras. In fact, it's straight out of *Sherlock Jr.* in which a dreamy projectionist walks into a movie through a screen. The main difference is that *Last Action Hero* had critics and audiences scowling, while *Sherlock Jr.* is widely regarded as a screen masterpiece."[16]

Keaton's enduring influence on filmmakers and moviegoers

around the world is now becoming better known. The Spanish surrealist filmmaker Luis Buñuel is quoted in the epigraph to this essay, and his admiration is apparent even in his first film, the still-surprising surrealist exercise made with Salvador Dali, *Un chien andalou,* completed just four years after *Sherlock Jr.* Buñuel ends his tale with a young woman and man sticking out of the sand on a beach, dead. The allusion is clearly to several of Keaton's endings, which make use of tombstones marking "the end" (*College* and the short *Cops,* for instance).

Consider a more recent example of Keaton's influence, the 1989 Academy Award–winning Best Foreign Film, Giuseppe Tornanoya's *Cinema Paradiso.* As the projection booth in the small Sicilian town cinema catches fire, the flames ignite the old movie images tacked to the wall. Among the chosen few photos is one of Buster Keaton, staring out at us with his "great stone face," his eyes both innocent and knowing, and completely silent. This brief moment occurs a third of the way through *Cinema Paradiso.* Surely most who enjoyed this film about film and the role it played for this small Italian community and, by implication, plays for us all missed the director's silent wink in including a Buster Keaton photo in the projection booth. With it, Tornanoya pays tribute to Buster Keaton as a great force in early cinema and particularly to *Sherlock Jr.,* the prototype for films about movie projectionists who mingle their dreams with those on celluloid and thus with the dreams of each audience member.

Joanna E. Rapf and Gary L. Green have written in their book, *Buster Keaton: A Bio-Biography,* that one of the twentieth century's most widely recognized playwrights, Samuel Beckett, was a great fan of Keaton's silent comedy, finally traveling to the United States in 1964 to direct him in a short film entitled *Film.*

Finally, the young Soviet filmmakers Sergei Eisenstein, Dziga Vertov, Pudovkin, and others made vast contributions to the development of film language in the 1920s as they combined their Marxist-communist revolutionary fervor with the avant-garde spirit of the times. Yet for all their experimentation and efforts to reach "the people" with their films, Soviet box-office records show that American silent comedy outsold all Russian films and that, of the silent stars, Keaton outsold Chaplin.[17]

More recently, Johnny Depp has given a haunting performance in *Benny and Joon* (1993) as a Keaton-like figure in contemporary America who is able to win the attention and then the affection of a deeply troubled young woman, in large part by acting out a persona modeled on Keaton. There is even a large photo of Keaton early on in the film and a number of gag references. But most of all, what finally reaches Joon is the gaze – that clear-eyed innocence that appears to know and yet still wonder at experience and that does not judge or criticize or humiliate. Ultimately, Benny's gaze, like Keaton's, not only draws us in, but is comforting on a comic level that is much deeper than that usually achieved by those who focus almost entirely on easy laughs. Few entertainers anywhere succeed this well, this long.

NOTES

1. Jean-Pierre Lebel, *Buster Keaton*, trans. P. D. Stavin (New York: Barnes, 1967), p. 16.
2. Robert Benayoun, *The Look of Buster Keaton*, ed. and trans. Randall Conrad (New York: St. Martin's Press, 1983), p. 157.
3. Ibid., p. 6.
4. Ludwig Wittgenstein, *Philosophical Investigations* (Oxford: Basil Blackwell, 1968), p. 195.
5. Quoted in John McCabe, *Mr. Laurel and Mr. Hardy* (New York: Grosset & Dunlap, 1966).
6. Milan Kundera, *The Art of the Novel*, trans. Linda Asher (New York: Grove Press, 1988), p. 65.
7. Quoted in Hal C. Herman (ed.), *How I Broke into Movies: Signed Autobiographies by Sixty Famous Stars* (Hollywood: Hal C. Herman, 1928), p. 207.
8. David Robinson, *Buster Keaton*, 2d ed. (London: Secker & Warburg, 1970), pp. 15–16.
9. George Wead and George Lellis, *The Film Career of Buster Keaton* (Pleasantville, NY: Redgrave, 1977).
10. Janes Agee, "Great Stone Face," *Life* 27 (September 5, 1949): 84–5.
11. Walter Kerr, *The Silent Clowns* (New York: Knopf, 1975), p. 25.

28   ANDREW HORTON

12. Daniel Moews, *The Silent Features Close Up* (Berkeley: University of California Press, 1977), p. 36.
13. Rudi Blesh, *Keaton* (New York: Collier Books, 1966), p. 244.
14. Kerr, *The Silent Clowns*, p. 224.
15. David Rodowick, "*Sherlock Jr.* Program Notes," *Cinema Texas* (University of Texas, Austin), March 3, 1977.
16. George Mannes, " 'Jr.' Achievement," *Entertainment Weekly*, January 21, 1994, p. 55.
17. Christopher Bishop, "The Great Stone Face," *Film Quarterly* 12:1 (Fall 1958): 20.

▌ "This Fellow Keaton Seems to Be the Whole Show"

BUSTER KEATON, INTERRUPTED PERFORMANCE, AND THE VAUDEVILLE AESTHETIC

Imagine two Introduction to Film courses. Prof. Old-man, a liberal humanist, has been teaching film for several decades, helping to introduce cinema studies at his university by crossing over from literature. His course stresses the formal and thematic "evolution" of film. Prof. Oldman wants his students to appreciate cinema's capacity to tell ever more sophisticated stories, to construct rounded characters, to engage in social criticism, and to achieve a high degree of "realism." Prof. Oldman's selections are works of formal "unity," "richness," "universality," and "profundity." Prof. Youngman, a lapsed leftist, came later, arriving with a degree in film studies from a major Midwestern university and a distrust of the "snares and deceptions" involved in classical narrative. Reflecting his ties to modernism, Youngman embraces "transgression," "excess," and "self-reflexivity," wanting a "countercinema" that calls attention to itself as a "constructed object" and that rejects the notion of "passive spectatorship."

One would anticipate that the films they choose to show their students are radically different. Prof. Oldman's syllabus is full of works by Griffith, Chaplin, Ford, Renoir, DeSica, Bergman, and

Truffaut. Prof. Youngman's course is dominated by Von Sternberg, Sirk, Arzner, Godard, Fellini, Oshima, and Fassbender.

Both professors teach Hitchcock, and both teach Keaton, though their choices of exemplary films reflect their larger aesthetic judgments. Prof. Oldman teaches *The General*, stressing Keaton's classicism, his willingness to subordinate isolated comic moments to a larger plot trajectory, his ability to motivate gags through a sympathetic understanding of his central protagonist, and his ability to speak both to a nostalgia for the nineteenth-century agrarian South and to contemporary anxieties about technology. Keaton is valued because he broke with the melodramatic excesses of Chaplin and produced more formally satisfying works. Prof. Youngman teaches *Sherlock Jr.* as a film that is profoundly aware of the institutions and practices of cinema, that forces the spectator to think about what it means to watch a movie and what place Hollywood fantasy plays in our lives. Prof. Oldman's Keaton the classicist bears little or no resemblance to Prof. Youngman's Keaton the modernist, and their interpretations and evaluations, no doubt, would allow for endless hours of debate at the faculty club. For Prof. Oldman, *Sherlock Jr.* is too fragmented, its image of a spectator penetrating the world of the screen a "parlor trick" that distracts from larger plot goals. For Prof. Youngman, *The General* is too staid and predictable, too much a part of the classical tradition.

In their search for the "essential Keaton film," both Profs. Oldman and Youngman distort the complexity of his place in film history. First, both men build a case for Keaton's "uniqueness" not so much by systematically comparing his works with the slapstick tradition as by pulling his films out of their larger generic context altogether. Neither seems especially interested in tracing the vaudeville tradition that Keaton's style of comedy came from or how it fit within larger production patterns in the silent cinema. Second, both view the Keaton features in isolation from his larger career trajectory – or more accurately, they see the other Keaton films, the "nonessential" ones, as "stepping stones" toward his "great achievements" or as marking his "swift and tragic decline." Neither his early shorts with Roscoe "Fatty" Arbuckle nor his sound features with Jimmy Durante warrant much more than a sneer, since these films do not exhibit his control over the production process. Third, their readings of the films in question depend on a simplification of their formal construction. Prof. Oldman's focus on narrative and character-ization requires him to read past gags that don't fit comfortably within the causal development of the film – or to dismiss them as undesirable excess.[1] Prof. Youngman's focus on the reflexivity of *Sherlock Jr.* often comes to rest on a couple of comic set pieces, while ignoring how those moments of disruption operate within the narrative. Keaton's films, like those of other slapstick clowns, struggle to resolve the tension between plot and spectacle, char-acter and performance, which are core concerns of the comedian comedy as a generic tradition.

All of this is to say that the choice of *Sherlock Jr.* as the focus of an anthology in the 1990s is a product of complex shifts within film studies as a discipline, shifts in aesthetic taste, profes-sional training, and ideological commitment that affect both what films we teach and what we say about them. For these reasons, it is important to understand why *Sherlock Jr.* incites our critical attention as probably the canonical Keaton film for the 1980s and 1990s. (*The General*'s decline in critical popularity is another story, which would require a different essay.) While we need to look closely at the aesthetic claims made for *Sherlock Jr.*, we risk duplicating the blindness of both Profs. Oldman and Youngman if we isolate the film from larger historical contexts. *Sherlock Jr.* came at a particular moment in Keaton's career and in the history of screen comedy, and to understand it we must broaden our framework, to make links between its moments of disruption, reflexivity, and spectacle, and the traditions from which it emerged.

To begin with, let us look at a point on which Profs. Oldman and Youngman (and, indeed, most film critics and historians) might agree: the centrality of Keaton as comic persona, comic performer, and comic filmmaker to our understanding of his feature films. The historic conditions that gave rise to this phenomenon, its aesthetic and thematic consequences, and its place within the larger history of classical Hollywood cinema are only beginning to be explored. This clown-centered style of slapstick represented a specific (and fleeting) moment in the development of screen comedy.[2] At the same time, the tension between performance virtuosity and narrative continuity, the grounds upon which Profs. Oldman and Youngman disagree, reflects the complex relationship of Keaton's features to larger shifts in film style throughout the early years of cinema.[3] A growing body of scholarship has focused on the transition between the "cinema of attractions," an early mode of film practice based on self-conscious spectacle and strongly inspired by vaudeville practice, and the classical Hollywood cinema, a subsequent mode centrally focused on narrative and influenced by traditions of theatrical realism.[4] The relationship between these competing aesthetic systems was dynamic, not static, shifting in response to changing production contexts and audience demands. Film comedy was particularly bound to the vaudeville tradition, which defined the "cinema of attractions," and was more resistant than most genres to the pull toward classical narrative.

The career of Buster Keaton, who began as a child star in vaudeville, traced the transitions in screen comedy throughout the silent era. Keaton started out as a bit player, or "second banana," with Fatty Arbuckle's comic troupe, reflecting the ensemble-based comedy style associated with early slapstick films, but he gradually gained greater screen time. Keaton's solo shorts, such as *The Play House*, required only a minimal plot frame, with most of the pleasure coming from spectacular sequences of virtuoso performance, stunts, or gags. Like those of his contemporaries, Keaton's silent features, such as *Sherlock Jr.*, drew on melodramatic conventions to give coherence and structure to their comic set pieces, responding, with various degrees of success, to demands for strong story logic and clear character motivation. The coming of sound provoked a reconsideration of the potential appeal of variety entertainment, resulting in a more fragmented, performance-centered style of screen comedy. Keaton negotiated this final transition with difficulty and only minimal success.

After a brief discussion of Keaton's relationship to the vaudeville tradition, this essay will look closely at four Keaton films, *Back Stage* (1919), *The Play House* (1922), *Sherlock Jr.* (1924), and *Speak Easily* (1932), which pose, in vivid terms, the tension between the vaudeville aesthetic and the classical Hollywood cinema. Specifically, I will focus on the various ways in which the four films facilitate and motivate extended sequences of performance virtuosity. Each film takes a playhouse or movie theater as its central location, and each represents as its central comic image the disruption or interruption of a performance (an image that can be traced back to "The Three Keatons" stage act). Each film invites our awareness of performance as performance, of the institutions and processes of show business, and of the construction and maintenance of social identity.

Looking at these four films suggests a new way of resolving the conflicting claims Profs. Oldman and Youngman would make about *Sherlock Jr.* and the other Keaton films. Prof. Oldman's account doesn't fully acknowledge the continued influence of the disruptive, nonlinear, performance-based tradition of vaudeville throughout Keaton's career. On the other hand, Prof. Youngman's account leads him to locate reflexive impulses at the very moment where Keaton's comedy seems most fully assimilated into the classical system and to find transgressiveness in elements that are highly conventional aspects of slapstick comedy. *Sherlock Jr.* is both more transgressive and more classical than our faculty lunchroom debates acknowledge, representing simply one moment in Keaton's lifelong negotiation between the competing aesthetics that shaped early film comedy. What will emerge is not so much Keaton the classicist or Keaton the modernist as Keaton the vaudevillian.

"THE THREE KEATONS" (1901)

Within months of his birth, Buster Keaton was appearing on stage with his parents, and by the age of five he had become the central feature of a popular vaudeville act. As Peter Kramer has shown, the addition of this child star was what his parents had long needed to make the transition from medicine shows and small-time variety shows to the big time – a novel twist.[5] The original Keaton act, "The Man with a Table," had adhered closely to the traditional formula for male–female comedy acts, combining Joe Keaton's acrobatic performance and broad comedy with Myra Keaton's "artistic" poses, dancing, and musical performance on various woodwinds. Without Buster, the Keatons had enjoyed moderate fortune. With Buster, the act became a popular success.

Not only was Buster younger than most child stars of the period, but his act offered a radically different picture of childhood. The most popular child stars typically embraced sentimental and melodramatic notions of childhood innocence and remained more or less passive spectacles within acts dominated by adult performers. Keaton's act, however, offered a more rambunctious and aggressive image of parent–child relations, requiring Bad Boy Buster's active performance. The mischievous child pretended to disrupt his father's act until Joe Keaton hurled the boy about the stage, dragging his head along the floor like a mop. At one point, Joe would toss Buster into the wings or into the orchestra pit, thinking he had at last cleared the way for a completion of his performance, only to have the boy returned by a thoughtful stagehand. "Is this yours, Mr. Keaton?" Joe often milked the laugh, slowly signing a receipt for Buster, before beginning to sing a song, which once again the boy would interrupt. The interrupted performance was a common act structure within the vaudeville tradition, seeming to hold open the prospect of onstage action as spontaneous, unrehearsed, improvisational. Vaudeville sought to maintain the illusion – and it was only partially an illusion – that the audience's responses shaped the performance.[6] In a theatrical tradition described by one Chicago critic as "the field of the expert," there was a certain pleasure in watching a performance go awry, witnessing events disrupt and threaten the performer's mastery over stagecraft, only to see order restored once again.[7]

Such knockabout antics integrated Buster fully within an act that had made its reputation for vigorous and acrobatic performance. Buster's contributions sometimes included singing songs, reciting "The Village Blacksmith," or doing impersonations of other popular performers. The specific content of the act varied as the Keatons toured the circuits – it was expanded, shortened, or altered to conform to the demands of specific venues – but the concept of an interrupted act and the slapstick treatment of the young boy remained the core around which other performance specialties could be structured.

In many ways, "The Three Keatons" epitomizes the vaudeville tradition. The underlying logic of the variety show rested on the assumption that heterogeneous entertainment was essential to attract and satisfy a mass audience. The vaudeville program was constructed from modular units of diverse material, each no more than twenty minutes long, juxtaposed with an eye toward maximum variety and novelty. Performers were responsible for originating their acts, negotiating with production specialists for materials and props, rehearsing and refining their performance skills, and transporting and maintaining scenery. Under these conditions, a family-based act like that of the Keatons was far from unusual, and it was possible, even necessary, for all members of the act to make creative contributions to its evolution.

This performer-centered mode of production resulted in an aesthetic strongly focused on performance virtuosity. Performers were expected to execute their specialties with a consistently high level of speed and precision. Frequently, acts were designed to draw attention to the performer's skills, having little or no other interest. Such was certainly the case with protean or quick-change acts, in which the star might perform an entire one-act play, alone on the stage, shifting gestures, vocal patterns, and

costumes to convey as many as forty or fifty different characters.[8] The young Buster's abilities as a prodigious child performer
attracted this same kind of fascination, with some critics specu-
lating that his feats could be performed only by a midget.

Vaudeville style was streamlined, stripped down to those elements most likely to provoke emotion, building toward a "wow
climax," a moment of peak spectacle calculated to ensure a final
burst of applause. Performers often directly addressed the audience or crossed beyond the footlights. Making little attempt to
preserve the invisible fourth wall that characterized theatrical
realism, vaudeville performers foregrounded the process of performance, often in highly reflexive ways, as when the Keatons
structured their performance around Buster's perpetual disruptions of his father's act and included orchestra members and
stagehands as part of the performance. Closely related to this
reflexive quality in vaudeville performance was what Neil Harris
calls the "operational aesthetic," a fascination with how things
work, with the mechanics and technology of showmanship.[9]

Vaudeville was not about telling stories; it was about putting
on a show and, more than that, it was about each performer's
individual attempt to stop the show and steal the applause.
Vaudeville had little use for the trappings of theatrical realism; it
was about the spectacular, the fantastic, and the novel. Vaudeville had little use for continuity, consistency, or unity; it was
about fragmentation, transformation, and heterogeneity. The
incorporation of this vaudeville tradition was what gave silent
screen comedy its intensity and fascination; it was also what
made the genre's absorption into the mainstream of classical
Hollywood cinema so problematic. Classical cinema, like theatrical realism, *was* in the business of telling stories, constructing
characters, maintaining continuity, consistency, unity, causality, and plausibility. Classical cinema, unlike vaudeville, sought
to efface the mechanisms of its production, presenting itself as a
coherent, self-contained world cut off from the realm of spectator experience.

BACK STAGE (1919)

One of the last of the fifteen two-reelers that Buster Keaton made as a contract player from Fatty Arbuckle's Comique Studios, *Back Stage* reflects the ensemble or "stock company" style associated with early slapstick comedy, something of a throwback to the techniques Doug Riblet associates with Mack Sennett's Keystone Studios in the early part of the decade. If Fatty Arbuckle was billed as the star attraction and constructed the film to showcase his talents, Buster Keaton's contributions had grown to the point that he could no longer justly be characterized as a "second banana," and Al St. John waited in the wings, stealing the spotlight at key moments with his own eccentric performance. Watching the film today, we are drawn to Keaton's stone face and his extravagant pratfalls, and especially to a series of mechanical gags that prefigure famous moments in Keaton's own star vehicles: the film's opening shows a bedroom that is quickly transformed into a stage when the walls are carted away, a comic surprise that Keaton will exploit in *The Play House;* a stage flat depicting the side of a house gets knocked over and falls directly onto Fatty, who passes untouched through the window, a moment that predates the falling house in *Steamboat Bill Jr.;* and Buster and Fatty take "shocking" revenge on an abusive strongman, electrifying his barbells, a gag that rehearses Buster's punishment of the rival electrician in *The Electric House.*

Retrospectively, *Back Stage* seems like Buster's show, but this is something of an optical illusion, a trick of historical consciousness. The film opens and closes on Fatty and it is Fatty who woos and wins the female lead, even if it is Buster who takes the more active role in overpowering the film's comic antagonist, the brutish strongman who seeks to disrupt their performance. Fatty may be the boss and Buster the assistant, onscreen and off, but Buster's comedy often hinges on his insubordination in upstaging his master.

Its theatrical setting allowing a constant exploration of issues of performance, *Back Stage* seems acutely aware of this struggle over the spotlight, exploiting it for comic variety and narrative conflict. A running gag has one performer after another demanding the "star dressing room" at this fleabag theater, with Buster and Fatty using a pulley to circulate the star among all of the dressing rooms. The star role similarly circulates, at times almost as mechanically, between Buster and Fatty. When Al St. John makes a memorable cameo appearance as an eccentric dancer, his rubber-leg contortions are framed by matching (but separate) reaction shots from Buster and Fatty. First Fatty and then Buster try to imitate St. John's performance with equally spectacular results, proving their own mastery over the bodily repertoire of silent slapstick. The effect is not unlike challenge dances in tap or improv sessions in jazz, where each performer seeks to match and top what has come before. Something similar occurs when first Fatty and then Buster confront the abusive strongman: Fatty's threatening gesture turns into a silly little dance, while Buster's attempts to bash him with an ax only seem to tickle him.

When the focus shifts from backstage preparations to onstage entertainment, the film allows Buster to perform a harem dance in drag, showing an unexpected grace and fragile beauty, only to be pushed aside by Fatty, dressed in a leopard-skin robe, who engages in a frenzied and equally show-stopping dance. Here, the two clowns achieve maximum impact by dancing together, the queen having caught "dance fever" and the king having "mistaken himself for an acrobat." At other moments, Buster threatens to upstage Fatty, as in the "Serenade in Snow" sequence, in which a bossy Fatty chastises Buster for not shivering in the cold and then chastises him again for overplaying his responses ("I said shiver – not shimmy!") or when Buster disrupts Fatty's big musical solo by accidentally knocking the backdrop over his head. The aggression reaches a peak when "Queen" Buster steals "King" Fatty's throne and then the possessive monarch picks her up and dumps her, unceremoniously, onto the ground. Seated at Fatty's feet, Buster disrupts the king's wooing by plucking hairs painfully from his legs, a gesture of aggression he tries to pass off as a sign of affection.

The constant one-upmanship between Fatty and Buster influences the rest of the characters, with the plot centering around a succession of theatrical rivalries. In the rough-and-tumble world of the Arbuckle shorts, the threat of assault and humiliation is never far from the surface. A sign posted on the wall outside one of the dressing rooms reads, "In bowing after your act, bow as low as possible. You can't tell what is coming!" St. John's expansive dance movements send one stagehand flying and he kicks the hat off Fatty's head. The other performers are shocked and outraged by the strongman's constant abuse of his female assistant, whom he makes carry all of the bags and arrange his weights. The group plots and schemes to teach him a lesson in chivalry, finally subduing him with electrified barbells. The strongman seeks revenge by calling the other performers out on strike, forcing Buster, Fatty, and the other stagehands to "improvise" a performance. St. John jeers the show from a boxed seat, until Buster, leaping into Fatty's awaiting arms, misses and crashes down on him. A stagehand, hanging from the rafters and sending fake snow onto the actors below, gets tired and dumps the whole bag on Fatty's head, and an angry Arbuckle strips off his coat and threatens to punch him. The strongman's attempts to disrupt the show prove even more aggressive, with boos turning into open violence; he pulls out a pistol and shoots the leading lady midperformance. Here, the comic violence of slapstick seems to push too far and more dramatic retribution is demanded. Buster grabs a trapeze, swings up into the balcony, and drags the bully back onstage, where the entire cast pelts him and finally drops a trunk full of weights on his head. If this disrupted performance and the resulting fisticuffs give the film its "wow climax," it must be followed by a more traditional resolution, where Fatty kisses the romantic female lead as she recuperates in the hospital, arbitrarily culminating a romantic subplot scarcely suggested by the preceding scenes. That the film spends so little time introducing or developing this relationship suggests Arbuckle's indifference to the trappings of the classical Hollywood narrative, the plot existing only to motivate and contain the sequences of comic performance.

If the professional competition/collaboration of Arbuckle and Keaton intensifies *Back Stage*'s entertainment value, the story suggests that professional rivalries between characters can only disrupt the show with escalating violence. As a director, Arbuckle seems to have been remarkably generous (or perhaps simply shrewd) in allowing his talented co-star to share so much screen time. As a character, Fatty seems to fight aggressively for control over the theatrical troupe, even if such control is always just beyond his reach. In the world of *Back Stage*, co-stars, though necessary, are also always potential competitors, and audiences, while necessary, are always potential assailants, with threats to the star's dignity and dominance coming from all sides. The trope of the interrupted performance serves to foreground the instability of ensemble comedy, while providing ample chances for each of the comic stars to showcase what they can do. One of Keaton's first independent projects, *The Play House*, by contrast, centers far more fully on the pleasures of virtuoso solo performance and the resulting problems in maintaining a stable character identity.

THE PLAY HOUSE (1922)

Buster Keaton buys a ticket to a vaudeville show. On-stage, he finds Buster Keaton conducting an orchestra of musicians, each of whom looks just like Buster. The curtain opens to reveal a minstrel show, a whole troupe of Buster Keatons who dance and crack jokes. The camera pans the audience to show a woman (Keaton in drag) and a man (also Keaton), both dressed in high fashion. Buster studies the program, "Keaton's Opera House. Buster Keaton Presents Buster Keaton's Minstrels." The camera slowly scans down the page, showing that all of the jobs are being performed by Buster's multiplying clones. Scratching his head, the gentleman remarks, "This fellow Keaton seems to be the whole show."

Paying homage to the vaudeville tradition of the protean act, *The Play House* allows Keaton to showcase his range as a performer, displaying his mastery over all of the stock characters of the vaudeville repertoire. Keaton plays musical instruments; he dances; he dresses in drag, as an infant, and as a trained monkey; he does acrobatics as part of a troupe of Zouaves; he mugs to the camera. He does all of this in a single film, often occupying multiple positions onscreen at the same time through his mastery of trick photography, so that he can subsequently settle down to one role and one identity (and some would argue, one plot) repeated over the rest of his career.[10]

The Keaton shorts only retrospectively seem like prototypes for the feature films, while, experienced in their own terms, they suggest a series of explorations and experiments into nonnarrative or seminarrativized structures. In his shorts, Keaton allows the vaudevillian's fascination with performance, spectacle, the "operational aesthetic" to outweigh the classical demands of storytelling and characterization. The shorts may parody other film genres (*The Paleface*) or transform the very notion of plausible causality into an absurd joke (*Cops*); they may play with theme and variation, systematically dismantling a previously ordered space (*The Blacksmith*), or trace the process of constructing and deconstructing a house (*One Week*) or a boat (*The Boat*). What ultimately matters, however, are not these flimsy structures but rather the gags and performances they imperfectly contain. Nowhere is that pleasure in performance as performance, as a disruption of characterization and a delay of narrative closure, experienced more fully than in *The Play House*.

From the outset, the film links Keaton's technical virtuosity as a filmmaker (the camera tricks that allow multiple Keatons to dance in precise synchronization within a single frame) with his mastery as a performer (his ability to become a whole theater full of different characters). Much as the vaudeville aesthetic pushed performers to encompass many different modes of entertainment within a single act, *The Play House* depends on a succession of protean shifts between different comic roles and different forms of showmanship.

At the same time, the film consistently returns to the image of the disrupted act, the performance that fails to proceed according to plan. Even in the opening dream sequence, in which "that Keaton fellow seems to be the whole show," the Keatons are not fully in control of their performances, as the conductor scratches a persistent itch with his baton or the musicians seem confused about how to play their instruments, as the various audience members squabble with each other and clumsily spill their drinks down each other's backs. As the film proceeds, Keaton's harried stagehand must struggle to avert disaster as one performance after another falls apart. The Zouaves go on strike, so he must try to transform a group of ditchdiggers into a drill team. Buster watches helplessly as they bungle action after action, mistaking a midget for a gun barrel, firing the cannon into their own ranks, and knocking over the wall they are supposed to climb. When Keaton tries to dress the ape in his tuxedo, the primate escapes and so Buster is forced to take his place, resulting in a dizzying layer of identities (a man pretending to be an ape pretending to be a man). Ultimately, this already unlikely impersonation dissolves into a man pretending to be an ape failing to imitate a man and giving way to his animal nature. Buster picks fleas, scampers about the stage on all fours, climbs into the audience to frighten a female spectator into a faint, and finally dives through the backdrop to escape punishment. His co-worker dons a fake beard, only to have it burst into flames, and the tank act starts to drown, requiring Buster to smash open the aquarium. Each sequence hinges on the liveness of theater, the possibility that anything that can go wrong will, and the need for improvisation to ensure that the show will go on no matter what.

The frenzy of performance seems to disrupt and destabilize everything here. The boundary between stage and audience space is highly permeable, with Keaton at one point hurled off the stage into the street, where he is forced to buy a ticket in order to reenter the theater. In the final sequence, Keaton floods the audience, forcing it to flee into the streets, transforming the orchestra pit into a swimming pool, which he rows across using a drum as a boat and a fiddle as an oar. Identity is wildly unstable. Gag after gag depends upon mistaken identity (his consistent inability to tell the twins apart), incomplete identity (a running gag about two one-armed men who must cooperate to applaud the performance), transformed identities (Keaton's impersonations of women, children, and animals), and multiple identities (a whole series of gags centering on proliferating mirrors). In the end, Keaton stands confused before his own reflection. Space is wildly unstable. At one point, Keaton as an audience member applauds a team of eccentric dancers, only to awaken in the next shot in his own bed, the whole act having been a dream. No sooner does he awaken, however, than people begin to move his furniture away and the entire wall of his apartment seems to collapse, turning out to be a theatrical backdrop, and he finds himself in the wings of the playhouse. He leans on his broom and falls through the floor. Nothing is stable, nothing coheres – until the film's final sequence, in which everything falls apart and everything comes together. As with so many of Keaton's shorts, we know where we are going only when we get there.

The twins, two beautiful women whom Keaton is incapable of telling apart, are first introduced as a running gag. One responds to Buster's romantic attraction with a kiss, the other with a slap, yet circumstances conspire to keep him perpetually confused about which is which. As *The Play House* progresses, Keaton moves back and forth between scenes involving his offstage confusion over the twins and scenes involving the disruption of onstage performances. The onstage acts are constantly changing, the episode involving the Zouaves following immediately after the episode involving the trained monkey, while the enigma posed by the twins recurs, Keaton's frustration escalating each time he is unable to distinguish between them. The film's conclusion involves two successive actions – the final disruption of the staged entertainment (the flooding of the theater) and the final stabilization of the twins' identities. Buster escapes from the flooded theater, dragging one protesting twin in tow to the justice of the peace. When he discovers his mistake, he races back to rescue the other, more willing woman and then, borrowing a paintbrush from a nearby workman, places a big X on her shoulder blade, at last fixing her identity, one stable point in an otherwise chaotic universe.

The flooding of the theater represents the kind of "wow climax" preferred by the vaudeville aesthetic, a moment of maximum spectacle and peak emotional experience. The scene at the justice of the peace, on the other hand, represents the classical closure preferred by the Hollywood cinema, at last resolving narrative enigmas and tying up the central plot threads. That both climax and closure must be present suggests the tensions that run throughout the film between audience fascination with virtuoso performance and spectator expectations of narrative coherence. Keaton's accomplishment is to forestall until the last possible moment the subordination of performance spectacle to narrative causality. With his move to feature films, the balance will shift in the other direction.

SHERLOCK JR. (1924)

Sherlock Jr., the world's greatest detective, the crime-crushing criminologist, displays a surprising character flaw. He needs to have things explained. Again and again, Gillette, his "gem" of an assistant, stops the action to show the preparations for a trick or to reveal his face behind a disguise. Elsewhere in *Hearts and Pearls,* the film-within-a-film, Sherlock Jr.'s deductive powers are unquestioned. He can seemingly read the suspects' minds, scrutinizing their features for uncomfortably long periods. He anticipates the exploding pool ball, dodges the poisoned drink, and toys with the booby-trapped chair. No matter what the trap, he escapes unscathed – partly as a result of his own brilliance as a descendant of the great Sherlock Holmes,

FIGURE 9
Buster, the small-town projectionist, stands before the ticket office, a shot that does not appear in the film. *Sherlock Jr.* (Courtesy of KINO Video, New York.)

partly as a result of sheer luck (that seemingly inescapable pun on his name). Yet at other moments, he is surprisingly imperceptive, confused by Gillette's ability to masquerade as a mustached policeman or an old lady. He needs to be shown the dress inside the hoop before he can do his miraculous transformation into an old woman.

Of course, we recognize that these explanations exist not for the character but rather for the audience, part of the process of letting us in on the trick. Keaton knows that even with all of the explanations, even when the transformation occurs before our eyes (complete with a cutaway wall on the cabin), we will never quite be able to figure out how he leaps through the window, passes through the hoop, and emerges on the other side clad in women's clothing. Even with all the forewarning, we will never quite determine how he is able to dive through the box at Gillette's midsection and disappear into the rotating wall behind him or how Gillette, fully materialized again, can walk away. Like a good magician, Keaton wants to show as much as he can so that we focus on how the trick might have been performed while withholding just enough so that we can never really understand how the mechanisms work.

In *A Hard Act to Follow,* the documentary on his life by Kevin Brownlow and David Gill, Keaton suggests that *Sherlock Jr.* originated from his desire to exploit "some of these tricks I knew from the stage . . . some of them are clown gags, some Houdini, some Shung Li Fou." On the vaudeville stage, however, a magician, like Keaton's old family friend Harry Houdini, would present these devices directly for our examination, would lift his sleeves to show us that there was no hidden trick. Here, however, operating within the classical cinema, Keaton cannot directly address the spectator and must instead cast himself as a diegetic observer for whom the trick must be explained before it can be performed. The contrivance doesn't quite work. We recognize that these devices are being laid out for our attention. If nothing else, the disappearing wall on the cabin tips the filmmaker's hand. Still, Keaton tries to fit his penchant for stunts and magic tricks within the rules and conventions of the classical film, to explain everything according to plot and character even as he focuses our attention on performance and spectacle.

In fact, Keaton performs two kinds of tricks in *Sherlock Jr.* First, there are the tricks he performs for the camera, his pool table tricks, his acrobatic stunts (including breaking his neck when water from a spout pours down on him, knocking him to the ground), his trick motorcycle riding, his quick-change act, and his demonstration of stock comic turns, such as the sticky paper act or slipping on a banana peel. Here Keaton wants us to watch his performance unfold in continuous space and time so that there can be no escaping our awareness of his mastery. Second, there are the tricks Keaton performs *with* the camera, special effects such as the doubling of Keaton as he slips into dream or the transformation of the cast of *Hearts and Pearls* into their real-world counterparts or editing tricks such as the rapid transformation of space as Keaton struggles to get a foothold in the movie world. Here Keaton wants us to be fully aware of the camera manipulation, to recognize that the camera can make us see things that could not possibly occur. (And, in some cases, as in the motorcycle riding, he freely mixes trick photography with actual stunt work so that it is hard to tell how much of what we see is really happening.) There is a certain contradiction, then, between Keaton's desire to impress us with the reality of what he can do in physical space and to fascinate us with the illusion of reality he can create through his manipulation of cinematic space. The fascination with his leap from manhood into womanhood lies in the fact that we can't be certain which form of trickery is involved: seeing is believing and yet, at the same time, what we are seeing is incredible, and that is the essence of magic (screen, stage, or otherwise).

Few can doubt that Keaton wants us to be acutely aware of the experience of watching a movie unfold. Critical analysis of *Sherlock Jr.* has always focused on its reflexive qualities. Walter Kerr, for example, writes, "*Sherlock Jr.* is, plainly and simply, a film about film . . . an almost abstract – though uninterruptedly funny – statement of shocking first principles."[11] Kerr finds it a highly self-conscious exploration of the differences between cinema and everyday experience:

Film's properties and man's properties are of contrary orders altogether. Man's presence in the universe . . . is a sustained one, continuous in time and space; film is discontinuous. Man's presence on earth . . . is organic, all of a piece; film is all pieces, broken, fragmented. Man's knowledge of himself is in great part a logical knowledge, moving in a linear fashion from cause to effect . . . film is arbitrary on all counts.[12]

Kerr's description is curious since, rather than identifying properties that separate lived experience from the cinema, he is really identifying the distinction between classical cinema and a more avant-garde film practice, between continuity editing and montage/collage. Without denying *Sherlock Jr.*'s impulses toward reflexivity, we must also acknowledge its impulses toward conformity to classical Hollywood norms, including those mandating continuity, coherence, and causality. All too often, the case for its anticlassical impulses comes down to a single sequence, the moment when Keaton tries to pass from the movie theater into the film itself and filmic reality gets destabilized, shifting from scene to scene with little narrative motivation, tossing Buster from a riverbank into a snowdrift. If, for a few moments, Keaton imagines a different kind of cinema, one governed by discontinuity editing, one built from clearly visible fragments, one joined together in a purely arbitrary fashion without regard to cause–effect logic, the film as a whole does not operate according to those principles. Once Buster has been absorbed into *Hearts and Pearls,* the film resumes continuity editing, follows a clear, conventional plot trajectory, with each part following linearly and logically from what has come before.

What is perhaps most striking about this justly celebrated sequence is just how difficult it is to penetrate the realm of the movies in comparison with the constant breaking of the "fourth wall" in *Back Stage, The Play House,* and *Speak Easily.* Buster must undergo a series of painful transformations before he can be fit to the demands of cinema – not the least of which is his acceptance of the plot's goals as a dictate on his own actions. Buster's intrusion into *Hearts and Pearls* is, in some senses, another interrupted performance – with one significant difference. When young Buster intruded into his father's vaudeville act, he could stop it in its tracks, change its shape and direction. When Buster, as the stagehand in *The Play House,* smashes open the glass and floods the theater, he again changes the performance through his actions. But, here, Keaton can do little to alter the forward momentum of the film. He is at the mercy of its movements; the form allows only limited room for improvisation. Buster can imagine himself the film's masterful protagonist, can read its characters in relation to his real-life experiences, but *Hearts and*

Pearls ends the same way (with the rescue of the woman and the consummation of their romance) whoever plays the lead.

Here Keaton expresses something of the uncertainties and ambivalence a vaudevillian must have felt toward this new medium. News reports described vaudevillians as confused and agitated when they stepped onto a film set, uncertain what audience to address, directing jokes toward the cameramen and thereby "spoiling" takes, looking into the camera and violating Hollywood's edicts against direct address. Vaudevillians had difficulty grasping the temporal and spacial separation between performer and audience as well as the need to reproduce the performance the same way for each take. If the point of the Keatons' stage act was that anything could happen once a child took the spotlight, the point of *Sherlock Jr.* might be the indifference of film to audience intervention and performer improvisation.

Significantly, of the four films, *Sherlock Jr.* is the only one that focuses on the mechanism of cinematic performance rather than theatrical performance. *Sherlock Jr.* is the film in which Keaton, as director, as performer, is most fully constrained by classical norms, consistently working to provide strong narrative motivation for each and every performance turn, slapstick bit, and spectacular stunt. From the opening scenes, the film introduces its protagonist's problems, the conflict between his ambitious fantasies (to become a detective) and his mundane real occupation (as a projectionist), the rivalry between Buster and "the local sheik" for the girl, and the barriers he faces in resolving these problems. What might have been treated as a random series of gags in one of the shorts – Buster's discovery of a dollar bill in a rubbish heap and its subsequent reclaiming by a beautiful if obviously deceitful woman, a sobbing older woman, and a street tough – is here given a tight narrative explanation. Buster needs three dollars to buy his girl a box of candy but has only two; with the extra dollar, he could make a good impression, but forced to fork over his own money to one of the claimants, he must settle for the one-dollar box. A minor deception, trying to pass the one-dollar box off as a more expensive selection, leaves him open to being framed by his rival and sets the whole story into motion.

In the next sequence, comic moments (his clumsy attempts at courtship) are consistently crosscut with more narratively significant ones (the sheik's theft of the watch, his exchanging it at the pawnshop, his purchase of the coveted expensive candy at the confection store, and his planting of the pawn ticket in Buster's pocket). Crosscutting, a mechanism of continuity, causality, and consequence, epitomizes classical narration, both pushing the event chain toward its inevitable resolution and reinscribing the links between otherwise isolated actions. Buster's courtship represents the culmination of one plot movement (the concerns about Buster's one-dollar candy box being sufficiently impressive to woo the woman) but also introduces a new problem (the theft of the watch), which threatens to further delay the romance's anticipated resolution. Buster's attempt to play detective results instead in his being identified as the thief and being forbidden by the girl's father to court her again. His desire to clear his name motivates an extended slapstick sequence as he pursues the sheik, which results only in his soaking himself. The girl, however, suspects something is fishy, goes to the pawnshop, and identifies the man who hocked the watch, thus holding open the prospect of a speedy reconciliation.

The introduction of the film-within-a-film structure forestalls such a simple and direct path toward closure, introducing a second plot that closely parallels the first. Again, jewelry is stolen, a woman threatened, and a detective called to solve the mystery. The use of a parallel plot allows Keaton to abbreviate the narrative exposition, but he is still careful to show us each step in the plot. *Hearts and Pearls* arguably has five movements: the theft of the pearls, Sherlock Jr.'s investigation of the scene of the crime (in which he narrowly avoids a series of attempts on his life), the recovery of the pearls and the uncovering of the villain's plans, the rescue of the girl, and their escape and romantic coupling. Each movement provides opportunities for Keaton to perform a number of spectacular stunts, often involving the transformation of his identity or a narrow escape from death. Rather than stopping the show, Keaton's ability to change his identity serves utilitarian purposes, allowing him to foil the villains and complete his narrative goals.

The most extensive performance sequence involves his cross-country ride on the handlebars of a runaway motorcycle during which he weaves in and out of cars, passes by a row of workers hurling dirt, rips through a tug-of-war and knocks aside picnic tables, and barely misses an oncoming train. If, as Don Crafton suggests, slapstick gags represent the "potholes" that slow and sometimes derail the forward momentum of comic chases, the chase here occurs at such a breakneck speed that it scarcely slows for the gags.[13] It simply rolls over them and keeps on moving. Buster's cycle approaches a tree lying across the road, but workmen blow it away with dynamite just before he hits it. Narrative logic is pushed to absurd lengths, as nothing seems to retard the protagonist's relentless and single-minded pursuit of his goals, and lest we miss the point, the film crosscuts to the villain accosting the girl, ensuring that every gag is read in terms of its narrative consequences.

Perhaps its most overt parody of the very idea of continuity comes when Sherlock, racing away from the villains in the final moments of the film, pulls out the exploding billiard ball, introduced, pocketed, and then forgotten in a much earlier scene, and blows them away. Classical to a fault, every detail counts, nothing can be excess, and so the exploding billiard ball will finally be rendered functional in terms of the plot. At the same time, however, the extreme delay between its introduction and its plot consequences renders the whole concept of narrative economy an absurd joke, resolving an enigma that the audience has long since forgotten.

This chase sequence can be interpreted as a parody of the silent serials in which chance plays a large role in the protagonist's escape from a cliff-hanging plight at the end of each chapter. Here, as in the serials, the protagonist cheats the viewers almost as much as he cheats death, and in this context the nonrealistic elements seem highly conventional rather than breaking the cinematic illusion. Sherlock's larger-than-life exploits are so exaggerated that it becomes hard to take them seriously and so we laugh at their improbability and excess. Yet, I would argue, our laughter does little to diminish our intense fascination with Sherlock's pursuit of the villain or our sense of triumph when he rescues the girl. The sequence draws its emotional force from the very plot conventions it parodies, just as the film as a whole both operates within and calls attention to the norms of classical narrative.

As with many comedian comedies, the film's narrative trajectory is a conservative one, bringing its protagonist into greater conformity with social expectations. Buster learns his proper place within the social order by imagining himself cast as a film protagonist and mapping his real-world problems onto the screen story. In his real life, Buster's attempts to become a hero are clumsy and ineffectual; he ends up being cleared of false accusations not by his own decisive actions or brilliant deductions but by his fiancée's feminine intuition. As Sherlock Jr., on the other hand, he takes charge of the situation from the outset and maintains control no matter what obstacles he encounters. The detective book, however useless in the real world, seems to have prepared him for the challenges he faces in the imaginary space of the cinema, while the cinema's instructions, in the end, may be what he needs to move from romantic ineptitude toward marital bliss. Performance thus allows Keaton to try out heroic and romantic roles and to master them. Just as *Sherlock Jr.* brings Keaton's fascination with performance in line with classical norms of story construction, the film also brings Buster's eccentric performance into conformity with the performance of socially expected roles.

However, as with many comedian comedies, this assimilation into social norms may be temporary and unstable, called into question by the final ambiguous gag in which Keaton either refuses or doesn't know how to fulfill the expectations of heterosexual marriage. The comedian comedy never fully embraced the closure characteristic of the classical cinema, allowing a degree of openness or ambiguity normally absent from the Hollywood film. On the other hand, since the move to assimilate the protagonist into the social mainstream gives this genre its core plot structure, some nod toward social acceptance is conventionally present, even if the final gag almost inevitably pulls the rug out from under narrative expectations. If *Sherlock Jr.* is a film about film, what it teaches us is the strategies by which slapstick comics sought to be assimilated into the mainstream of the classical cinema, strategies that subordinate comic spectacle into narrative exposition, even as the film wants to exploit our fascination with the extraordinary technique of its star performer. By the early sound period, the relations between performance and narrative would shift once again, but by this point Keaton seemed unable to make this transition to a looser, more flamboyant style of performance.

SPEAK EASILY (1932)

The opening-night performance is a shambles. Chaos reigns onstage and off. Each time the professor (Buster Keaton) tries to put things right, he makes things worse, knocking dancers from their feet, getting roped and spun around by his feet from a moving cyclorama, tripping into the orchestra pit and being shoved back onto the stage again. With each catastrophe, he offers a mild-mannered apology to the audience for "a slight departure from the routine of this section of the entertainment." But the far from disgruntled audience laughs, applauds, celebrates each disruption, and the show is a triumph. A Broadway veteran, having seen the show in rehearsal and judged it a failure, berates the director, "Why didn't you tell me that the professor was a comedian?"

The showman's confusion is understandable. Little in the film up until that concluding sequence would give anyone much cause to believe that Buster Keaton is a comedian. Few critics have written about Keaton's sound comedies, and those who have pass over them quickly amid the tragedy and pathos of Keaton's offscreen problems, his financial difficulties, his alcoholism, his declining control over his own career. If we look closely here, we can see scenes that were obviously flubbed because a drunk Keaton was unable to deliver his lines, moments where he can't hold his head steady, his voice wavers, and his eyes refuse to focus. Lines are muffed, gags fall flat, pratfalls are clumsily presented, and perhaps most tellingly, one of the film's primary set pieces is strung across a number of quick cuts, suggesting that it was pasted together in the editing room. This marks quite a fall from Keaton's famous long-take, distant camera approach, which sought to preserve and display the integrity of his most spectacular performances. But in *Speak Easily*'s final moments, Keaton returns yet again to the motif of the interrupted performance with spectacular results. As the professor loses control, Keaton gains his old footing.

Far from a throwaway line, the opposition between the professor and the comedian is basic to the film. In the early sound period, MGM sought to revive Keaton's sagging screen career by casting him against Jimmy Durante, then the studio's most promising comic performer. Durante's style was loud and vulgar; his delivery was quick and excessive, providing a sharp contrast to the restraint most often associated with Keaton, whose carefully modulated voice ideally suited his "stone-face" image. At times, Keaton plays straight man for the hyperbolic comedian, yet at its best moments, the film depends on the stark contrast between two distinctive comic styles. Early sound comedy had embraced such eclecticism, striving for a blending of different comic styles, of alternative forms of entertainment, in the hope of creating something that might appeal to both urban sophisticates and small-town audiences. Taking its lesson from vaudeville itself, the early sound period wanted to package heterogeneous material for a heterogeneous audience, while somehow shoehorning the mix into conformity with classical norms of storytelling and characterization.

As Professor Post, Keaton plays a man fundamentally out of touch with the world around him. In the opening scenes, his valet tells the professor that he approaches the same fate that befell his predecessor, a man who committed suicide because he had "lived alone with his nerves" for so many years. The valet urges the professor to "go out and find life," but the professor wants to save his money for a rainy day. "It rained the day they buried him," the valet warns, before producing a letter (later revealed to be a forgery) informing Post that he has inherited a small fortune. The mythological inheritance liberates Post. Where, moments before, his movements were lethargic, the professor now bursts into action, frantically packing his bags, bouncing through the doors and windows, at last ready to confront the world: "I'm going some place. I just don't know where yet."

Durante, on the other hand, plays Jimmy, a down-and-out comedian traveling with the flea-bitten Midnight Maids Company Theater, constantly only one step ahead of bill collectors and town sheriffs. When Durante makes his first appearance, Jimmy's performance skills are being called into question: "You haven't got a gag that would get a giggle." When Jimmy first encounters the professor, it is in a painful attempt to prove to his critic that he *can* get laughs, but the literal-minded academic keeps missing the point and foiling the punchlines, offering new twists on otherwise stale jokes. "It was too subtle," Jimmy protests. "It went over his head like a trapeze." Twice in the film, Durante is shown performing before totally indifferent audiences, his desperate attempts to entertain falling short of the mark.

Much of the film's comedy centers around the unsuccessful attempts of the two men to bridge the great cultural gulf between learned professor and lowbrow comedian. Jimmy speaks only in slang, while the professor's speech is pretentious, convoluted, and arcane. At some points, communication breaks down completely as Jimmy spews forth a string of vernacular synonyms until Post begs, "Can someone tell me what he's trying to say?" It is the professor's stodgy attempt to correct the slang term "speak easy" with the more grammatically precise "speak easily" that gives the film (and the play within the film) its title. Keaton's character has "learned everything except how to live." Durante's character, on the other hand, needs to have someone "tone you down and polish you up."

In the end, *Speak Easily* does not so much revitalize Keaton or refine Durante as find in the blending of the vulgar and the arcane the perfect material to satisfy a jaded Broadway audience. Considering the need for comedy, the professor proposes that they might "take a lesson from the Greeks," borrowing material from Aristophanes. Citing a succession of fads in show business involving exotic material (such as Hawaiian hula dancers), Durante suggests that Greek material might have calculated ethnic appeal: "There's a million Greeks in New York! I'll take somethin' from 'em." When the professor instructs the chorus girls on how to do "authentic" Greek dancing, the dance comes out looking more like the shimmy, though he suggests to the shapely Thelma Todd that "it would be more effective if you performed it in the nude." For once, the professor's ideas are too lively for Jimmy, who as a seasoned vulgarian knows how far to push over the line: "They might get away with that in Athens. That's a college town."

Itself something of a patchwork of borrowed material, *Speak Easily* takes much of its plot structure from the backstage musical. Gags and one-liners compete for screen time alongside the struggle to put on the show, the constant threat of failure, and the romantic rivalry between the seductive (and scheming) Eleanor Espiere and the decent and good-natured Pansy Peets. Here, as in *Sherlock Jr.*, classical norms hold sway, motivating the comic action, while, in this case, robbing it of much of its punch. Exposition often surfaces in plodding and mechanical ways in early sound comedies, as if it has had to be severely compressed in order to make way for the spectacular performance sequences. The more attention the film pays to this often-formulaic plot development, the more pedestrian it starts to seem, with the absence of solid character development allowing little or no interest to develop around the twists and turns of the story.

However, in the film's closing moments, performance set pieces displace the forward progression of the plot, at last offering a space where Keaton can engage in broad slapstick. Eleanor (Thelma Todd) lures the professor back to her apartment, planning to seduce him and force him to marry her, serving him a Tom Collins to set the mood. The teetotaling professor quickly develops a taste for the drink, which, avoiding as always the vernacular, he calls "Thomas Collins," and so he mixes the next round of drinks even stronger, resulting in a slippery mess. Keaton and Todd fall all over each other, their limbs twist and tangle, their bodies flip, flop, and fold. Ironically, given Keaton's offscreen alcoholism, drinking "Thomas Collinses" seems to emancipate the professor from his constraint and free Keaton to do his performance tricks. Eleanor directs the action, having already scripted the evening so as to trap the "wealthy" professor into marriage and having arranged for a male actor to play the part of her outraged brother. Yet her attempts to stage-manage the affair fail, since the professor doesn't understand his role, doesn't deliver his lines, and eventually turns the show into a crazed farce. Durante arrives just in time, trading places with the confused professor. When the outraged "brother" delivers his melodramatic denunciation of Todd's moral downfall, Durante steps onto the stage proclaiming himself her suitor and vowing marriage. As a result, the entire scene goes nowhere – at least as far as plot consequences are concerned. But the comic spectacle of Keaton and Todd groping at each other offered its own rewards for pre-code audiences.

At the opening-night performance of "Speak Easily," narrative order is further fractured to make way for broad slapstick spectacle. Post has played the part of a rich Broadway producer without realizing that his inheritance is a fraud and he has no money to pay his bills. Jimmy seeks to keep the professor away from the bill collectors long enough for the show to open and perhaps recoup its costs. The professor, for his part, wants to ensure a smooth performance, but his unfamiliarity with stage routine and his own absentmindedness create disorder every time he seeks to restore order.

If, in *Sherlock Jr.*, Keaton twice gets expelled when he tries to pass through the screen into cinematic reality, nobody can stop Post from wandering past the curtain and into the show, even when they tie him to the flies. No clear-cut barrier separates onstage from backstage. Keaton may bound all over the stage, even swooping down on the show from the rafters, but the world of the stage remains separate from the space of the spectators, preserving the fourth wall that was so consistently violated in *The Play House*.

The film in *Sherlock Jr.* is relentlessly plot-driven, suggesting the narrative commitments of the classical Hollywood cinema, but the Broadway revue in *Speak Easily* is resolutely non-narrative, a string of musical numbers offering up constant spectacle and novelty but little plot. Keaton's disruptions only intensify the fragmentation and eclecticism of the variety show. His accidental comedy draws loud laughter from the theater audience (which thinks the professor is part of the show). When Jimmy tries to do his rehearsed performance, he doesn't get a single laugh, but when Post's erratic and confused behavior encourages him to improvise on stage, Jimmy also becomes a comic hit. His vaudeville skills allow him to react quickly and capitalize on each catastrophe. When a humiliated Eleanor storms offstage following her disrupted number, Jimmy puts on drag and shamelessly mugs onstage, while Post romps around him. Here Keaton and Durante offer audiences two kinds of performance and two kinds of comedy.[14] Keaton's comedy centers around an inability to conform to social expectation, a comedy of accidents and ineptitude, while Durante's comedy is more aggressively anarchic, marking a conscious break with social expectation and a pleasure in its own rambunctiousness.

This elaborate set piece provides the kind of "wow climax" anticipated by the vaudeville aesthetic and the anarchistic comedy typical of the early sound period. The film moves Keaton from a stifling order (where his inability to act in the world leads toward loneliness and death) toward the moment of peak chaos and confusion (where his actions enliven an otherwise predictable performance). Yet to read *Speak Easily* as simply another anarchistic comedy is to misread the paradoxical status of this performance, since its point is precisely to use disorder to clear the way for a new order, somehow turning a disastrous failure into the basis for a stage (and screen) success. Jimmy finds the audience approval he so desperately seeks. The producer who once scorned the show leaves it impressed. The bill collector walks off with the new backer, who is promising to put his real fortunes behind the show. The professor at last acts upon his love for Pansy and at the same moment learns to use slang, telling Eleanor, "Nuts to you." Despite some anarchistic tendencies, *Speak Easily* still embraces the comedian comedy model, still wants to operate as fully as possible within the demands of the classical cinema, still provides a strong sense of closure. At the same time, the film's narrative, no less than the stage show, gets derailed by excessive performance sequences. Insofar as the comedy works, it works in opposition to rather than in the context of plot logic. Ultimately, however, performance sequences are pulled back into narrative logic and become instrumental for plot resolution.

CONCLUSION

Writing in the *New York Times,* modern-day comic Bill Irwin, whose Broadway shows have been read as a return to the Ziegfeld and vaudeville traditions, spoke of his admiration for Keaton's silent comedy: "What's the blend that makes Buster Keaton's physical comedy so wild and so visceral but at the same time so finished, so sure?"[15] Keaton, Irwin argues, was both a gifted acrobat, whose remarkable performance sequences provoke the awe of contemporary performers ("Take care in viewing this part with dancers: They often want to rewind and watch it again and again"), and a gifted actor, who knew "how to harness the story-telling potential of acrobatic movements." For Irwin, the comic highpoint of Keaton's career was his monkey impersonation in *The Play House*, a set piece that perfectly illustrated his performance skills, yet Irwin also admires *Sherlock Jr.* as a film that more perfectly subordinated gags to larger narrative contexts: "These gags and stunts and bits are, with Keaton, almost always memorable episodes in tightly told story. . . . That's what he and Chaplin were best at: stories that don't feel episodic even when they're woven from little comic turns." Irwin assesses Keaton as a fellow craftsman, someone who appreciates both the vaudeville stage traditions and the classical Hollywood traditions that shaped his work. His account of *Sherlock Jr.* sees it as a perfect balance between the two.

For many other critics, like the hypothetical Prof. Youngman, *Sherlock Jr.*'s bid for canonization hinges on its reflexive qualities, properties that set it apart from dominant Hollywood practice. Unlike the other Keaton features, it does not simply tell a classically constructed story but rather offers a meditation on how classical stories are told. *Sherlock Jr.*'s film-within-a-film structure invites audience awareness of cinema as a set of institutions and practices, as a technology of showmanship and storytelling. Yet we need to be cautious in ascribing to the film a modernist sensibility. To do so is to isolate these moments from their broader historical context(s), to reduce *Sherlock Jr.* to a series of set pieces without considering how these seemingly transgressive moments operate within the film as a whole, how they fit into Keaton's career, or how they relate to the complex interplay between vaudeville and classical traditions. We need to recognize the classical impulses that Irwin praised in his discussion of the film.

Far from transgressive, the self-conscious display of performance was a conventional aspect of American slapstick, a holdover from the vaudeville stage where showmanship took precedence over storytelling and performers invited audience awareness of their performance skills. As we move from the canonical works of Chaplin and Keaton to the forgotten comedies of minor clowns such as Lupino Lane and Raymond Griffith, the display of performance as performance becomes more pervasive. What separated the classic silent comedies from the bulk of slapstick films was not their reflexiveness but their conformity to classical norms, their ability to couple spectacular performance with melodramatic story lines so that each gag had plot consequences and was motivated in terms of the characters, their goals, and their conflicts. In doing so, they traded the advantages of one aesthetic tradition for those of another, a shift that need not be understood simply in terms of a progressive mastery over the techniques of cinematic storytelling, as Prof. Oldman would no doubt have it, or of a selling out of counter-cinematic impulses, as Prof. Youngman might protest. The embrace of classical conventions does not come without a loss of spontaneity and virtuosity, of the freedom of the performer to display the full range of his or her talents, or of the unpredictability of a style of comedy that could take off in any direction. What it gained, perhaps, was a sense of narrative consequence, emotional resonance, and social import. Rather than choosing sides, valuing narrative over spectacle or spectacle over narrative, we might opt out of the debate, recognizing the relative strengths of *The Play House* and *Sherlock Jr.* as embodying differing aesthetic sensibilities, each with their own appeals, each with their own merits. Placing the films in a historical framework does not mean we have to buy into models of progress or of decline; we simply recognize the nature of the changes that are occurring. The reflexivity of *Sherlock Jr.* was not so much a radical departure as the last gasp of a style of comedy disappearing from the screen, not to resurface again until the coming of sound triggered a new phase of formal experimentation. What replaced it was a more narrative-and-character-centered style of comedy, one that gained greater critical acceptance, if not always audience popularity, as it sought a closer relationship to dominant Hollywood practice.

The motif of the interrupted act surfaces yet again in the final moments of Chaplin's *Limelight* (1952). Here Chaplin and

Keaton appear together onscreen for the first time, playing two former music hall stars brought out of retirement for a charity benefit. By this point, Keaton is a fading star, brought back through Chaplin's charity, while Chaplin is himself acutely aware that his own heyday is past. Like much of this film, their performance together is ripe with nostalgia. Even Keaton grumbles about the constant references to "old times." Their act involves a musical recital that goes progressively awry, material clearly closer to Keaton's oeuvre than Chaplin's. Chaplin insists on hogging both the camera and the spotlight, giving himself the broad rubber-legged comedy while Keaton is reduced to fumbling with the sheet music and reacting to Chaplin's antics.

Yet it is significant that, having chosen to include Keaton in the film, Chaplin saw this image of the disrupted performance as evoking his own comic legacy. In *Limelight,* the narrative clearly demarks times and places where performance spectacle can occur, motivating it in terms of the plot, the story of the last days of a once-great music hall performer. Chaplin allows the performance to be completed, smoothly, as it had been done so many times in the character's past, but as Chaplin is hurled from the stage into the orchestra pit (repeating, consciously or otherwise, Keaton's experiences in "The Three Keatons"), he injures himself. Sadly, Chaplin's character dies in the wings, bringing this tragic comedy to its inevitable ending. If the assassination of the actress in *Back Stage* was played for comic effect, Chaplin's death is pure pathos, a melodramatic tribute to the clown's professional commitment to seeing that the show goes on no matter what the cost, anticipating a similar death scene at the climax of John Osborne's *The Entertainer.* Anything but a disruption of the film's plot, the performance provides the necessary context for its resolution, the plot simply having stalled long enough for us to mourn the passing not only of a performer but of a whole style of performance.

Far from unique to *Sherlock Jr.,* the motif of the disrupted performance runs through Keaton's work, starting with his earliest stage appearances in "The Three Keatons," recurring in his shorts, silent features, and early sound comedies, and reprised with nostalgia relatively late in his career. Each time this image resurfaces, it suggests something slightly different. In "The Three Keatons," the disrupted performance centers around a particular conception of the bad boy as aggressive, unpredictable, and spontaneous. Here the disrupted performance created excitement by suggesting the unpredictability of live theater, its responsiveness to audience enthusiasms and unexpected turns of events. In *Back Stage*, the disrupted act invites an awareness of the comic ensemble as an unstable blending of distinct personalities, showing both the potential collaboration and the potential competition between talent. In *The Play House*, the disruptive performances fit within a thematic of destabilized and transformed identities, allowing us to celebrate Keaton's ability to take on and discard an array of stock theatrical roles. Here, the non-narrative pleasures in performance virtuosity exist on an equal footing with our hunger for narrative coherence and resolution. The final disruption of the stage performance paves the way for closure as Buster and his lover escape from the playhouse into marriage. In *Speak Easily*, the disrupted performance breaks down the barriers between sophisticated and lowbrow performance, between the professor and the clown, and between success and failure. The disrupted performance is at once an anarchic celebration of liberating disorder and the mechanism by which the film moves toward closure, resolving one by one the problems confronting the protagonists.

In many ways, *Sherlock Jr.* is the most aesthetically conservative of all of these films, allowing the least space for transgressive performance, demanding the greatest conformity to plot logic and narrative progress. The message seems to be that it is impossible to stop or transform a cinematic narrative once it is set into motion. In "The Three Keatons," *Back Stage*, *The Play House*, and *Speak Easily*, Keaton could stop the show or improvise in response to changing situations, while in *Sherlock Jr.*, the film moves relentlessly, ceaselessly toward its prescribed destination, and Keaton, unable to steer his own course, can only grab hold for the ride.

NOTES

1. For a critique of this traditional dismissal of unmotivated gags, see Donald Crafton, "Pie and Chase: Gag, Spectacle and Narrative in Slapstick Comedy," in *Classical Hollywood Comedy*, ed. Kristine Karnick and Henry Jenkins (New York: Routledge, Chapman & Hall, 1995), pp. 106–19.

2. The earliest comedies centered around anonymous pranksters, stock comic characters rather than recognizable comic performers. The development of more complex film narratives and the emergence of the star system resulted in an increased focus on comic performers as extratextual personalities appearing in film after film, but not necessarily on solo performance. Sennett's Keystone comedy, for instance, depended on comic ensembles, spreading the comedy throughout the entire cast. Comic teams are far more common in sound comedian comedy, while screwball or romantic comedy has tended to focus on complementary male and female co-stars. The emergence of the great clowns, then, was not an inevitable consequence of screen comedy but a particular manifestation of the slapstick tradition. See Peter Kramer, "Vitagraph, Slapstick and Early Cinema," *Screen* 29:2 (Spring 1988): 101–3; Tom Gunning, "Crazy Machines in the Garden of Forking Paths: Mischief Gags and the Origins of American Film Comedy," in *Classical Hollywood Comedy*, ed. Karnick and Jenkins, pp. 87–105; Doug Riblet, "The Keystone Film Company and the Historiography of Early Slapstick," in ibid., pp. 168–89.

3. For a fuller discussion of those shifts, see Henry Jenkins and Kristine Brunovska Karnick, "Acting Funny," in *Classical Hollywood Cinema*, ed. Karnick and Jenkins, pp. 149–67.

4. The concept of the vaudeville aesthetic is explored more fully in Henry Jenkins, *What Made Pistachio Nuts? Early Sound Comedy and the Vaudeville Aesthetic* (New York: Columbia University Press, 1992). The concept of classical Hollywood cinema is discussed most extensively in David Bordwell, Janet Staiger, and Kristin Thompson, *The Classical Hollywood Cinema: Film Style and Mode of Production to 1960* (New York: Columbia University Press, 1985).

5. I am strongly indebted to Peter Kramer for allowing me to use material from his manuscript in progress, *The Making of Buster Keaton: Slapstick, Stardom and American Popular Entertainment*. Most of the information included here about "The Three Keatons" is derived from Kramer's painstaking and invaluable reconstruction of Buster Keaton's stage career.

6. For a fuller discussion of vaudeville as a performance tradition, see Jenkins, *What Made Pistachio Nuts?*

7. "New Material Necessary Says Chicago Reviewer," *Variety*, October 5, 1917, p. 5.

8. Keaton would draw on this fascination with protean performance in *The Play House*, which similarly allowed him to play all the parts and to display his versatility as a comic performer.

9. Neil Harris, *Humbug: The Art of P. T. Barnum* (Chicago: University of Chicago Press, 1973), pp. 57, 72–89. See also Charles Musser, *High Class Moving Pictures: Lyman H. Howe and the Forgotten Era of Traveling Exhibition, 1880–1920* (Princeton, N.J.: Princeton University Press, 1991). Gunning, in "Crazy Machines," applies this concept specifically to Buster Keaton's screen comedy.

10. See, e.g., Daniel Moews, *Keaton: The Silent Features Close Up* (Berkeley: University of California Press, 1977).

11. Walter Kerr, *The Silent Clowns* (New York: Knopf, 1975), p. 227.

12. Ibid., pp. 228–9.

13. Crafton, "Pie and Chase."

14. Joanna E. Rapf, "Buster Keaton and Jimmy Durante: Mesh, Match or Blend?" (presented at the Society for Cinema Studies Conference, New York, 1995), examines more closely the ways in which *Speak Easily, The Passionate Plumber,* and *What No Beer?* combine and balance the clown comedy of Durante (with its focus on antisocial and unassimilated impulses toward pleasure and disruption) and the comedian comedy of Keaton (with its push toward conformity with the demands of the social order). Drawing categories from *What Made Pistachio Nuts?*, Rapf sees these films as a permutation of the "comic romance" tradition, though she suggests that the Keaton–Durante vehicles "do not fit into any of the categories" of early sound comedies described in the book. These categories were not intended to be mutually exclusive. Rather, they simply point toward potential plot structures during a period of experimentation, plot structures that were often mixed, matched, or merged in unexpected ways. As *Nuts* argues, the disruptiveness of anarchistic comedy was often balanced with a more integrative

plot, centered around uniting young lovers or saving the stores owned by older maternal figures. The romance of Professor Post and Patsy Peets, which serves to pull Keaton back into the social order at the end, is consistent with the romantic subplots found in many of the Marx Brothers films. In fact, Keaton's role closely parallels that played by Bert Wheeler in many of the RKO Wheeler and Woolsey comedies.

15. Bill Irwin, "Beauty in Form, and Even in the Face," *New York Times,* July 2, 1995.

PETER F. PARSHALL

2 Houdini's Protégé

BUSTER KEATON IN *SHERLOCK JR.*

There was indeed – and entirely apart from
nostalgic memory – something of the marvelous about vaudeville. It was so magnificently
irrelevant, so unpredictable, a kind of stream
of consciousness of the theatre. Everything
was thrown together – a dozen or more entirely different acts rushing one after the
other out on the boards until the stage was as
full of marvels as a vaudeville magician's silk
hat. . . . It was a glorious and preposterous
hodgepodge with a happy madness all its
own.

(Rudi Blesh, *Keaton*)[1]

The marvelous world of vaudeville was the only one
Buster Keaton knew from the time he was born until he began
making films. According to popular accounts, a backstage trunk
served as his crib and at nine months of age he interrupted his
parents' act by crawling onstage.[2] He soon became the mainstay
of that act and eventually propelled it into headliner status.
With no formal schooling and only an occasional summer away
from the circuit in later years,[3] Keaton considered the entire

67

world a stage, and his imagination was shaped by the whirl of acts that went on before his eyes. He watched these acts closely, for survival in vaudeville depended on adjusting to changing locales, changing audiences, and changing times. When Keaton moved from vaudeville to film, he carried with him not only the plots and gags of his earlier life, but also its sense of magical transformation.

Keaton was particularly fascinated by stage magicians. In its early years, the Keaton family worked together for some time in a traveling medicine show with Harry Houdini, who supposedly gave the young Buster his name when the six-month-old infant tumbled unhurt down a flight of stairs. Houdini remarked to Joe and Myra Keaton, "That's some buster your baby took."[4] Keaton reported that "Houdini showed me a few of his sleight-of-hand tricks" and added:

> No one, by the way, ever worked harder than I did to figure out Houdini's tricks. I watched him like a hawk every chance I got. I studied his act from all parts of the theatre, from both wings of the stage, from the orchestra and both sides of the balcony and gallery. I even climbed high up in the flies so I could look straight down on him as he worked.[5]

He admitted, however, "I found out nothing."[6] Keaton started playing at being Houdini when he was only six years old, doing a burlesque onstage of Houdini's famed escape from a straitjacket by putting his own jacket on backward and wriggling out of it with appropriate facial grimaces. Magic tricks appear in a number of Keaton films, such as the scene in *Steamboat Bill Jr.* (1928) in which Willie flees into a theater to escape a cyclone, jumps onto a small platform, and finds a bell pull hanging in front of his nose. When he pulls it, a curtain drops around him, then pops back up to reveal an empty platform. Willie then reappears through the trapdoor in the floor of the platform: it is a magician's apparatus, its secret revealed.

Magic tricks are especially evident in Keaton's 1924 feature, *Sherlock Jr.* Rudi Blesh terms the film "magical,"[7] and that word, although intended to express its impact on the audience, in fact captures its essential nature. Keaton specifically indicated that the film's central inspiration was the desire to reproduce some of the illusions he had seen on the vaudeville circuit:

> Some of these tricks I knew from the stage. I got that batch of stuff together but I couldn't do it and tell a legitimate story because there are illusions, some of them are clown gags, some Houdini, some Shung Li Fou. *It's got to come in a dream.*[8]

Sherlock Jr., then, is explicitly indebted both to the magician and to dream. While Keaton reveals the tricks behind some of his illusions in the film, in other cases he is delighted to leave us baffled. The most notable magic in the film is the young movie projectionist's ability to invade the space of the movie screen and transform himself into a marvelous detective in order to win back his girl. The boy as prestidigitator can transform his own body, the people around him, and the events of his life, forcing reality to conform to his wishes. Stirring together vaudeville's marvelous transformations, the magician's sleight of hand, and the wish fulfillment of dream, Keaton concocts his greatest illusions in *Sherlock Jr.,* a film that lifts the audience, like its hero, out of the everyday world. As much as any filmmaker since Georges Méliès (a practicing magician himself), Keaton sensed the potential of the film medium to transform the quotidian into the marvelous.

THE TRANSFORMATION OF REALITY

If Keaton brought with him from vaudeville a sense of the marvelous, film was the perfect medium through which to express it. Vaudeville's cousin, the English pantomime, had become particularly noted for its creation of spectacular illusions, with elaborate scenery changes and stage machinery to allow characters to fly to the moon or sail across oceans.[9] While vaudeville, with its succession of short acts, could not accommodate such elaborate stage illusions, the rapid progression of acts in itself provided a sense of a magical space that could be transformed completely from moment to moment. "In the end," Jenkins writes, "what vaudeville communicated was the pleasure of infinite diversity in infinite combinations."[10] Some sense of this magical diversity can be found in Keaton's 1922 short, *The Play House*, set in a vaudeville theater. The show opens with Buster making up the entire orchestra – playing all the instruments and acting as conductor. In the next scene, he is shown sleeping in a small room, and an angry man strides in, rousts him from his bed, and demands that he vacate the premises. A moment later, the "bedroom" vanishes, its walls carried away by stagehands and hoisted into the flies. Buster, it now appears, is only a theater worker being bawled out for sneaking a nap on the job. This playful shifting of identity and reality is one of the signal qualities of Keaton's comedy.

Sherlock Jr. gives a hint of the magical transformations that will occur by opening in a movie theater, but the shot is the reverse of what we expect, pointing toward the rear of the theater rather than at the screen, where the magic of the movies occurs. Having begun by looking in the wrong direction – at reality rather than into the cinematic world – the film remains obstinately stuck for the next several scenes. Instead of a mystery to solve, the budding young detective has a pile of trash to sweep up. Instead of finding treasure, he ends up giving away the dollars he needs to buy candy for his girl. Instead of sweeping her off her feet, he courts her awkwardly and then is thrown out of her life completely because of the machinations of his rival. He seems to exist in a space hostile to magic. All this changes when, a third of the way into the film, the camera points toward the movie screen, which our hero promptly tries to enter. It is the open door into a magic realm. Just how magical it is the boy soon discovers as he tries to invade that space, for it can shift its boundaries in the blink of an eye. The camera then slowly tracks forward, merging the borders of this world with the frame of the "ordinary" world we have been living in up to this point, carrying us like a magic carpet into the realm where miracles can happen. By denying his audience the magic of the film world in the first third of the movie, keeping us locked in the quotidian world, Keaton teasingly reminds us how much we desire the escape this realm provides.

THE MAGICAL ESCAPE

The film announces its intention to be a magic act from the first by its emphasis on escape. Houdini was renowned for his escape tricks, freeing himself from handcuffs, straitjackets, and locked boxes. In one of his famous stunts, the Chinese Water Torture Cell, his feet were fastened into stocks and he was suspended upside down in a locked cage, which was itself suspended in a glass-fronted water tank. He would emerge from the tank in two minutes. Similarly, a major motif in *Sherlock Jr.* is the magical escape. In the first part of the film, the boy tails his nemesis, the sheik, who sees him and locks him in a boxcar. A moment later as the train begins to pull away, the boy pops out of the top of the car, an action emblematic of the entire movie. He then runs along the top of the boxcars as the train picks up speed and, when he arrives at the last car, leaps to a water spout, which lowers him to the ground, but in a considerably dampened condition.

When the boy is magically transformed into Sherlock in the second half of the film, the escapes become even more marvelous. Locked onto a roof by the villain, Sherlock deftly grabs a train-crossing gate and lowers himself from the roof to the back of the villain's car. He deliberately allows himself to be dragged into the hideout of the thieves, much as Houdini would allow himself to be chained and padlocked. Inside the hideout, the villain shows him another detective, a less successful escape artist, who is held in an iron cage suspended from the ceiling. Pointing to the hapless victim, the villain threatens Sherlock, "When he's dead, I'll put you in there." But Sherlock is far too clever, and leaps through the window a moment later, snatching the stolen pearls as he does so, managing to pass through a heap to emerge fully dressed as a woman. He escapes again from a dead-end alley by leaping *through* the body of his assistant, Gillette, and escapes from his next pursuer on the handlebars of a motorcycle. Then, when he has rescued the heroine from the villainous butler, he escapes with her through the window just as the rest of the gang pulls up, and he thwarts their pursuit by blowing up their car with a dynamite-filled billiard ball. Houdini would certainly have been proud of his protégé's ability as an escape artist.

These escapes are paralleled by the film's movement from closed-in spaces to open ones. The film begins in restricted spaces – the back of the theater, the sidewalk in front of it, and the girl's parlor.[11] Although banished from the house when the girl's father tells him, "I'm sorry, my boy, but we never want to see you in this house again," the boy is also freed to the outdoors. His body seems to respond to this freedom by moving with far more agility as he tails the sheik. The suppleness of his movement creates a sense of kinesthetic freedom in the audience as time and again he narrowly misses running into the backside of his nemesis. This pattern is repeated in the second half of the film, which again begins in a theater (as the boy tries to invade the screen), moves to a domestic space (the mansion where the pearls have been stolen) and finally outside once more as Sherlock Jr. pursues the villain. Here the movement is even more expansive, with Sherlock riding in the back of the villain's car, escaping from the thieves' hideout, escaping a second time when trapped in an alley, and finally riding to the heroine's rescue on the handlebars of a driverless motorcycle. The camera work emphasizes this sense of more expansive space. In the interior scenes it is completely static. An action as simple as the boy's walking from the front of the theater to the candy store next door is shown in a cut. Then the camera switches to tracking to keep up with the boy as he shadows the sheik, and does so again as, in the second section, he rides in the rear of the villain's car. Finally, it absolutely races to keep up with him on the motorcycle. Keaton thus creates a marvelous sense of freedom through the expanding space of the action, the increasing pace, the moving camera, and the dangers to which the hero must respond with split-second reactions. The film's central movement, therefore, is from an ordinary boy trapped in narrow spaces in a quotidian world to an extraordinary hero who throws off every shackle with laughable ease and moves at will through the magical world of film.

DREAM MAGIC

At the core of Keaton's transformation of the boy and his world is the film's exploration of the dream realm. Freud's *The Interpretation of Dreams* was first published in 1900, the same time the motion picture was being invented and the movie camera was commonly designated "the dream machine" in recognition of the fact that it provided wish fulfillment, the dream's primary function.[12] In "Keaton Through the Looking-Glass," Garrett Stewart argues that Keaton's films in general and *Sherlock Jr.* in particular analyze "film's abiding bond to dream." Stewart suggests that it is appropriate for the boy to fall asleep on the movie projector, because it then projects "the imposition of his own unconscious fantasies upon the preternaturally receptive plot of the film actually being shown to the theater audience," becoming a "true dream machine."[13]

The film, then, follows the typical pattern of dreams that are populated with people from our own lives by having people from the boy's life replace the characters in the film. The first transformation shot has the heroine and the villain standing side by side. They slowly turn their backs to the audience simultaneously, then turn again, transformed into the boy's girlfriend and the sheik, who has outmaneuvered him. This turning exactly parallels the boy's first entrance into the girl's house, when the two of them walked away from the camera toward the stairs side by side, he holding his hat and the box of candy behind him. The two then turned slowly and shyly in opposite directions to face the camera. In both cases, the newel post is directly

FIGURE 10

Buster, in his dream, gets ready to enter the screen of the movie theater in which he works. *Sherlock Jr.* (Courtesy of the Academy of Motion Picture Arts and Sciences, Los Angeles.)

behind them and the stairs go up right in the rear. In the first scene, the boy follows the girl into the parlor; here, the sheik follows her up the stairs. A second transformation shot has the heroine's father metamorphose into the girl's father. The other characters from the boy's life also reappear in new guises: the handyman becomes the butler, evil henchman of the villain, and the theater owner becomes Gillette, Sherlock's assistant.

Not only are the characters the same, but the boy's attempted invasion of the movie screen obviously replays his earlier unsuccessful courtship of the girl. The events are condensed, following Freud's principle that dreams contain just key images to represent more complex thoughts and emotions.[14] In the film's opening, the sheik led the girl into the dining room and shut the curtains in the boy's face; here in the interlude, the villain locks himself and the heroine into a room. Just as the boy had sat disconsolately in the living room on the couch while the sheik romanced the girl in the dining room, here the figure of the dreaming boy sits in the theater audience and observes the villain attempting to kiss the heroine. Earlier, the boy had marched into the dining room only to be shown the door by the sheik; here, he is bodily thrown out of the movie scene. There, the boy slipped on the banana peel he had intended for the sheik and took a spectacular fall. Here, he tries to reenter the screen and takes a whole series of spectacular falls as the movie scene shifts around him.

Other iconic elements from the first scene reappear in subsequent moments of the film-within-a-film. The father announces the theft of the pearls standing in a doorway just as he did when he revealed the theft of his watch in the opening, with the girl, the sheik, and the handyman/butler gathered around. Although the setting is much more opulent, similar curtains frame the doorways in both scenes.[15] The only changes are that the mother is missing (she will become the maid in a later shot) and the doorway is not the one to the dining room but to the stairway. We also see the sheik slip the pearls to the butler as before he had slipped the pawn ticket into the boy's pocket. The two villains overhear the father calling Sherlock Jr. just as the sheik had looked over the boy's shoulder to see him reading his detective's manual. The number of parallel elements in the two scenes makes it evident that the film-within-a-film is intended to be the boy's dream reliving of his real-life events.

Particularly important is the way the beginning of the dream sequence captures the structure and the emotional tone of a dream, notably in the two scenes where the boy tries to enter the movie screen. For one thing, the illogicality of the action and the rapid changes of location suggest a dream's structure. More important, as Garrett Stewart has perceptively observed, the various scenes can also be read as a series of visual metaphors for the boy's personal situation, of the sort found very often in dreams.[16] After first having the father slam the house door in his face (a reminder of his having been shown the door at his girl's house),[17] he "finds himself figuratively swept off his feet, kicked out into the street, left high and dry, thrown to the lions, in a rut, at sea, all wet, and out in the cold." These images all show his "fears of rejection."[18] Overall, the scene-shifting episode continues the pattern already established, with the boy as completely helpless in the movie world as in the real world. The fade to black that ends this sequence, with the boy's dream figure sitting sprawled on the ground in a garden after his latest tumble, shuts him out of the dream world as completely as he is shut out of his girl's home. Thus, the film successfully captures many elements of a dream, with the characters and events reflecting the boy's life, the illogicality suggesting dream structure, and the events also capturing the boy's emotional state of rejection.

THE HERO AS MAGICIAN

The boy himself, on entering the film dream world, clearly lacks the power to affect it; the events of his life replay themselves with an outcome as depressing as in the film's opening. Everything changes, however, when the boy reappears in his new guise. When Sherlock Jr. first appears in a silk hat and tails, he could as easily be a magician as a detective, and in fact he plays the former role more than the latter. In his hands, all the elements of the boy's life are transformed. The boy's broom – symbol of his menial status and awkwardness (that piece of paper gets stuck to it) – becomes Sherlock's elegant cane and then the pool cue that he handles with such adroitness. The boy's porkpie hat becomes Sherlock's top hat. In several of his films, Keaton plays an upper-class person, as in *The Navigator* (1924), where he must transform himself from ineffectual snob to capable ship's steward. Here Keaton transforms himself before our eyes from awkward boy to sophisticated detective, reinforcing our sense that we could play the roles we see onscreen. We too could become rich and suave and omniscient at the blink of an eye.

Besides these external trappings, Sherlock transforms his very body. The boy was clumsy both physically and socially. He seemed to have no talents at all, good enough to be only a theater sweeper-upper, and ineffective in even that lowly occupation when confronted with a single sticky sheet of paper. His physical clumsiness was even more evident in social situations, as he hid his box of candy awkwardly behind him, sat stiffly beside his girl on the sofa, and slammed his hand down on top of hers. His awkwardness continued to be apparent as he took a tumble on his own banana peel and, when the theft of the father's watch was announced, searched the family members without confidence. Sherlock, by contrast, exhibits complete physical control – standing erect, moving confidently, looking people fiercely in the eye, and handling objects with complete assurance. His display of physical control culminates in the daring ride on the motorcycle, which Sherlock controls (albeit unknowingly) while seated on the handlebars of the driverless vehicle. That ride seems even more magical when it becomes evident that – in most of the shots anyway – Keaton actually was steering the motorcycle while seated on the handlebars.[19]

Not only has Sherlock Jr. transformed his body, but under his controlling wand the boy's dream film is now replayed and transformed from failure to fantasy triumph. Sherlock is welcomed by the family (whereas neither mother nor father had said anything to the boy during his courtship of the girl), seems to understand the crime completely (the boy had been at a loss), and successfully avoids the traps set by the pair of villains (the boy had been duped). Moews points out that Sherlock looks into the mirror over the pool table, watching the villains behind him, whereas the boy had missed a similar opportunity to look in the mirror over the fireplace and catch the sheik planting the pawn ticket in his pocket.[20] Sherlock's tailing of the sheik again results in his clumsily bumping his nose when he follows too closely, his being spotted by the villain, and his being trapped momentarily. The difference is that Sherlock is able to escape after the door to the roof is closed after him. His lowering himself on the railroad gate parallels the boy's lowering himself on the railroad water tank spout, but with far more success. The parallel shadowing is accentuated by the camera tracking left in both cases to follow the sheik tailed by the boy and the villain in his car carrying Sherlock unseen in the rear seat. One particularly interesting parallel is that both detectives end up being doused – the boy by the water spout, Sherlock when the car sinks in the pond at the end. As Stewart notes, "The dream has not after all won free of life's limitations, for once again Buster is 'all wet as a detective.' "[21]

The extended sequence of Sherlock Jr. playing pool is especially notable for establishing the detective's superhuman talents, using a technique that anticipates James Bond by several decades. Ian Fleming almost always includes a sequence in each novel that demonstrates the amazing skill of Agent 007 – such as the meticulously described golf game at Royal St. Marks in *Goldfinger* – so the audience accepts the conceit that Bond is skilled at *everything*. Likewise, the pool sequence shows Sherlock hitting a series of incredible shots, done without trick photography, including splitting away a pack of balls without moving the 13 ball that is set to explode, missing it by fractions of an inch, even curving balls around it or getting them to hop over it. (Blesh describes the trouble that Keaton took to actually sink those shots without using tricks,[22] in contrast to James Bond, who was always aided by camera manipulations and stunt doubles.) As much as from the shots themselves, we sense Sherlock's expertise from his dexterity in handling the cue. The scene climaxes when Sherlock takes careful aim at the deadly ball, then sinks it in a corner pocket with a sharp smack, slaps his cue on the table, and saunters out of the room between the two dumbfounded conspirators. As we (and they) learn a moment later, Sherlock has switched balls, pocketing the explosive one. But we are as surprised as they because they were watching his every move, lurking outside the doorway to avoid the coming explosion. We, likewise, had the sense of seeing every shot, with Sherlock at one point taking three shots in a row. This control of the world transforms him from ideal detective to miracle worker.

The sense of Sherlock's magical control of the world around him is signaled most notably in the following scene where Sherlock primps in front of a mirror – and then steps calmly through it. It is actually a doorway and we were tricked into believing it was a mirror by the placement of furniture in the same positions on both sides of the opening. Stewart considers this a key moment: it suggests that Sherlock, the mirror image of the boy, can penetrate any space. "Having once changed through the mirror of cinematic art . . . all mirrors, ordinarily as opaque and impenetrable as a movie screen, are opened to him."[23] Kerr agrees that this signals a turning point in the film. "All barriers are down. The business of 'going through' becomes the visual keynote of the balance of the film."[24] More examples of Sherlock's magical control follow in quick succession. He rides the railroad gate to land precisely in the back seat of the villain's moving car. Dragged into the thieves' hideout, he doesn't seem to notice that one of the thugs is stealing his watch, but then calmly offers to trade it for the thug's watch, which he has managed to lift without any of them (or us) seeing him do it. His escape from the thieves' lair, even though it is made "transparent" to us, amazes us with its deftness, as Sherlock snatches the pearls from the villain, dives through the window, and instantly transforms himself into an old woman in one unbroken movement. The miracle quotient escalates further as Sherlock dives through his assistant, Gillette, an act that is no longer rationally explicable but, as Stewart and Kerr suggest, follows "logically" from his walking through the mirror.

Sherlock's magical control of the world culminates in his ride on the motorcycle. He wreaks considerable havoc on passing vehicles and pedestrians and gets a half-dozen shovelsful of dirt in the face when he rides past a line of ditchdiggers, but time after time the world seems to operate as he wishes, like the cherry tree that bowed down to offer its fruit to the Virgin Mary as she carried the Christ Child. His motorcycle swerves through several busy intersections, but no car touches him. He races through a picnic, becoming a third contestant in a tug-of-war, and drags the last two warriors into a stream. He races along a bridge with a gap too large to leap, but two trucks on the ground below obediently drive forward from opposite directions, their tops filling in the missing space and allowing him to cross. The bridge is incomplete at the far end and Sherlock appears about to hurl into space, but the bridge gently sinks down, depositing him safely on the road. A tree blocking the road explodes to make way for him, an apparently solid vehicle lets him ride through its hollow middle, and a freight train speeding toward a crossing lets him pass in time. This last event stands in particular contrast to the way trains treated the boy – with boxcars trying to crush him, a locomotive spraying steam on him, a boxcar imprisoning him, and a water tower dousing him. Sherlock, by contrast, controls his world as magically as he controls the motorcycle. He speeds unerringly toward the shack where the heroine is imprisoned (even though its exact location is unknown), catapults precisely from the motorcycle, flies arrow-straight through the window, caroms across the table like one of the pool balls from the earlier scene, and drives the evil butler through the opposite wall in a shot as emphatic as his final sinking of the fatal 13 ball. The beautiful precision of his actions evokes a physical joy: human bodies are not earthbound after all, but, like angels and acrobats, are able to dance and whirl and fly.

THE MAGICIAN'S ASSISTANT

Other than Sherlock, most of the characters simply play more refined versions of themselves in the dream story, but there are two notable exceptions. One is the father's handyman, who is transformed into a butler, the villain's accomplice. This transformation is particularly striking, because the title that introduced the handyman emphasized that he did nothing at all: "The girl's father had nothing to do, so he got a hired man to help him." The evil butler, by contrast, is very active, becoming the *diabolus ex machina* of the film. It is he rather than the sheik who prepares the various traps for Sherlock – the poisoned drink, the falling halberd, and the explosive billiard ball. It is also he who apparently kidnaps the heroine, for we see him carrying her into the shack. And it is he who takes on the most villainous role of all, moving toward the terrified girl with a leer on his face and ominously (if somewhat comically) loosening his tie. The importance of his role is emphasized by the violence with which he is dispatched, as Sherlock knocks him clear through the wall of the shack. In the dream film, the innocuous handyman has become a co-villain of the sheik, as if a doubled version of evil were necessary to counterbalance the miraculous Sherlock.

But if evil is doubled in the dream film, so are the forces of good. Indeed, Sherlock's ability to transform himself and his world is matched or possibly exceeded by his assistant, Gillette – "A Gem who was Ever-Ready in a bad scrape," as the titles punningly identify him. He is played by the same actor who appears as the movie theater owner in the opening, angrily scoffing at the boy as he reads his book on how to be a detective. "Say – Mr. Detective – before you clean up any mysteries – clean up this theater." He is seen only once more, exiting the theater as the boy tries to get a piece of sticky paper off his hand. Absorbed in counting theater receipts, he does not notice as the boy plants his hand on the ground alongside the exit, allowing the manager to step on the pesky piece of paper and walk off obliviously with it stuck to his shoe. Thus, in the opening he is an authority figure, hostile to imagination and adventure, caught up in the pedestrian world of money making, and good only as the butt of a prank.

In the film-within-a-film, this figure, like the boy, is totally transformed. Whereas before he was the boy's boss, now the roles are reversed and he is the assistant. He is seen for just an instant as Sherlock dresses himself at home before going out to follow the villain. Gillette stands behind him, holding Sherlock's cane, but then is left behind as Sherlock walks out the door of a safe and onto the street. No words are exchanged, but apparently none are needed, so complete is their understanding of one another. Just as Sherlock seems to know instinctively where to go to intercept the villain, so a moment later Gillette appears even more magically. As Sherlock rides off in the rear seat of the villain's car, unseen by the villain, the camera that has been tracking alongside the car drops back enough to reveal a mysterious figure, its face turned away, clinging to the spare tire, unseen by the villain or Sherlock. This figure, we will learn in a moment, is Gillette. We thus marvel at Sherlock's deft insertion of himself into the villain's rear seat via the crossing gate, but marvel even more at how Gillette has inserted himself with still greater deftness, for we have not seen it occur.

When the car arrives at the thugs' lair with its two stowaways, Sherlock ducks out of sight as the villain gets out of the car; then, catching sight of the strange character behind him, he bops him with a pistol and leaps over the back of the car to hold him at gun point. The character pulls off his cap and false mustache to reveal himself as Gillette, who has somehow changed from the dark suit and four-in-hand tie he wore at Sherlock's place into a light suit, vest, cravat, and touring cap. From Sherlock's surprise, it is evident that this occurrence is not part of *his* plan, but is Gillette working on his own. Gillette is not some magician's assistant, handing over the props on cue and having no idea how the trick is done. Rather, he seems almost to be running the show. He ducks back to the car and brings Sherlock the round box he carried, and Sherlock opens it to reveal a woman's dress. Now understanding what is to be done, Sherlock arranges the dress back inside the box, sends Gillette running off (we presume to surround the house), and places the box in the window of the hideaway. Sherlock will dive through it a moment later, turn instantly into a woman, and make his escape unnoticed while the thieves mill around in confusion. But though Sherlock makes the precise dive through the box, snatching the stolen pearls from the villain as he does so, and nicely counterfeits the walk of an old woman, it is Gillette who appears to have planned the escape in advance. Furthermore, the cutaway shot of the hideout has revealed how Sherlock performed his trick of vanishing in an instant. We still don't know how Gillette appeared on the rear bumper of the villain's car.

Gillette's magic continues as, a moment later, Sherlock's disguise is penetrated by one of the thugs, who chases him into a blind alley. There appears to be no escape. But then Gillette appears a second time, this time popping up from behind a large box at the end of the alley. He has managed to change costume and location as completely and rapidly as Sherlock, for he is now dressed as a peddler woman carrying an open case of trinkets suspended from his neck. Again he directs the action, walking to the wooden fence at the rear of the alley, turning, and pointing to his sample case with both hands, signaling to Sherlock that this is his escape route. Sherlock hesitates only an instant and then, as two thugs close in on him, turns and takes a running leap through Gillette's case to vanish again. Gillette then walks calmly past Sherlock's stunned pursuers feigning puzzlement, shows them that his case is empty, turns to show that there is nothing in back of him, and calmly walks off, leaving them to stare at the empty alley. One whirls completely around in bewilderment. A moment later, the pair of thugs discover a gate in the alley fence and go through it; Sherlock exits neatly as they enter and locks the gate, trapping them. For all of Sherlock's deftness, however, Gillette appears the more magical figure, seeming to have arranged everything ahead of time, to have disguised himself in an instant, and to have appeared exactly when and where Sherlock needed him.

This process is repeated a third time, when Sherlock is running down the street a few moments later, having been discovered and pursued again by one of the thugs. The thug drops back from his pursuit when a motorcycle policeman in goggles rides alongside Sherlock as he is galloping full tilt down the street and stops him, pulling out a pad as if to write him a citation for speeding. Sherlock identifies himself by showing his badge; the motorcycle cop reveals himself by pulling off his false mustache: it is Gillette – again! In an instant he has gotten ahead of the racing Sherlock, changed costume for the third time, procured a motorcycle, and arrived exactly when needed. Then in an instant Gillette has vanished again, thrown off the motorcycle when it goes over a bump, leaving Sherlock unknowingly to pilot it from his place on the handlebars. Although we see the bump and see Gillette deposited on the ground as the motorcycle races off, this too is magical in a way, for it leaves Sherlock to receive full credit for rescuing the girl although he clearly could never have done so without Gillette's assistance.

Unlike the docile Dr. Watson, who served as plodding, puzzled amanuensis to the original Holmes, Gillette seems always to be several steps ahead of his master. He is a magical doppelgänger, appearing where he is needed and able to shift his shape at will. Just as he stood behind Sherlock, mirroring him as he dressed, so he mirrors him in the subsequent scenes. He is in motoring costume as Sherlock rides in the car, then in woman's dress to mimic Sherlock's quick change, then in motorcycle uniform – the personification of justice speeding to the rescue – as Sherlock sets out to save the girl. He twice appears wearing a false mustache just as the boy was first shown wearing one as he read his detective's manual in the theater. In a final mirroring, Gillette ends up sitting in a puddle as the motorcycle speeds away, finishing his scene all wet just as the boy in the railroad yard and Sherlock floating with the heroine in the car both ended up in water. He has moved to the opposite pole from his first appearance in the film, when he scoffed at the boy, ordered him about, and was unaware of the paper stuck to his foot. Now he sacrifices everything for his master, is all knowing and all prepared, and helps create a magical realm where the boy can be the perfect detective. Rather than scoffing at illusion, he becomes a master magician himself, dazzling the audience with his prestidigitation. For all the brevity of his appearance in the film-within-a film, his transformation is possibly even more miraculous than the boy's. Just as Sherlock Jr. serves as the boy's dream alter ego, Gillette seems to be a kind of dream alter ego for Sherlock. He is a fairy godfather, helping to transform the boy's pedestrian world into a magical realm in which dreams come true. If not only protagonists but ordinary people can be completely changed, then anything is possible.

The word "magic" has a variety of connotations, almost all of which are captured by this film. Magic can be sleight of hand, and this is suggested by Sherlock's instantaneous transformation into an old woman. Magic can include the miraculous escape, like Houdini's, from all restraints. Just as the boy escapes initially from the boxcar, Sherlock later frees himself from a succession of traps. The importance of this motif is emphasized by the movement into more expansive spaces and the freer camera tracking. Magic can include transformations, as when the magician turns a bouquet of roses into a dove. Here both scene and character are transformed, as the boy invades screen space. Magic can suggest thought processes of hallucination and dream, and the film's various transformations all suggest dream work, with the boy's rejection from the movie screen reminiscent of his expulsion from his girl's house. Magic, in particular, suggests a world whose operating principle is wish fulfillment. In the film, accordingly, the boy's body becomes a supple machine and the world conforms exactly to his wishes. Those around him are also transformed, with the handyman become a doubling of the villain and Gillette changed from scoffer to facilitator of detection. The quotidian world becomes the realm of magic as smoothly as the camera tracked forward to merge the spaces of the film and the film-within-a-film. Anything is possible here, on Keaton's stage "full of marvels."

CONCLUSION

Aristophanes' famous play *The Birds,* a key exemplar of comedy, emphasizes the freedom central to the form. Its hero and his friend, tired of political life in Athens, climb to the kingdom of the birds and convince them to build a city in the sky, Cloud-Cuckoo-Land. This city blocks the flow of smoke from animals sacrificed to the gods on Mount Olympus. The gods, who depend on the smoke for sustenance, are starved into submission and forced to sign a peace treaty that includes marriage of the hero to a beautiful goddess. Lehmann suggests that this magical kingdom serves as a paradigm of the freedom offered by comedy in general, "where all the hampering forces are abolished, where not only lovers but every man is free and winged."[25]

Such freedom is also evoked by *Sherlock Jr.,* which transforms reality and expands into the world of dream, dissolving our sense of what is logical and what is real. As Moews says, the viewer is so confused by the mixture of reality and dream in the film that he or she, like the boy in the film, is "wonderfully boggled, stunned by an illusion that seems, impossibly and simultaneously, both real and dream."[26] Like the heroes of Aristophanes, the boy is able to break free of the shackles that confine him and make everything in the world bend to his will. This is the realm of magical innocence we all desire, where everything accords with our wishes. If there is any limit to the film's festivity, it occurs in the ending, when the boy scratches his head at the image of the screen couple with a suddenly materialized family, as if unsure he wants to carry the festivity *that* far. Overall, however, this is one of Keaton's most triumphant films, not only in his mastery of the film medium and of his body, but in the picture of life it presents. Life's mysteries can be solved, reality can sometimes accord with our dreams, and – most important – there is more magic in the world than we realize. Included in that magic, one might note, are twins that instantly materialize on their father's knee, a neat trick indeed.

NOTES

1. Rudi Blesh, *Keaton* (New York: Collier Books, 1966), p. 39.
2. Tom Dardis, *The Man Who Wouldn't Lie Down* (New York: Limelight Editions, 1988), p. 1.

3. Blesh, *Keaton*, pp. 45, 64–6.
4. Ibid., p. 4.
5. Buster Keaton with Charles Samuels, *My Wonderful World of Slapstick* (New York: Doubleday, 1960), pp. 26, 51.
6. Ibid., p. 51.
7. Blesh, *Keaton*, p. 242.
8. Kevin Brownlow and David Gill, *Buster Keaton: A Hard Act to Follow*, three video tapes (London: Thames Television PLC, 1987).
9. M. Wilson Disher, *Clowns and Pantomimes* (New York: Benjamin Blam, 1968).
10. Henry Jenkins, *What Made Pistachio Nuts? Early Sound Comedy and the Vaudeville Aesthetic* (New York: Columbia University Press, 1992), p. 63.
11. Kevin W. Sweeney, "Parody and Comic Revision in Keaton's Features" (paper delivered at the Society for Cinema Studies Conference, New York, March 1995), p. 110.
12. Sigmund Freud, *The Interpretation of Dreams*, trans. James Strachey (New York: Avon Books, 1965), chap. 3.
13. Garrett Stewart, "Keaton Through the Looking-Glass," *Georgia Review* 33:2 (1979): 349, 352, 363–4.
14. Ibid., pp. 350–61.
15. Daniel Moews, *Keaton: The Silent Features Close Up* (Berkeley: University of California Press, 1977), p. 88.
16. Freud gives many such examples of metaphorical images in dreams. In one, a woman dreamed of a man standing on a tower, which represented her sense that he *"towered high above"* others (*Interpretation of Dreams*, p. 378).
17. It is worth noting that the heroine's father, who rejects the boy, is actually Buster's own father, Joe Keaton. For an interesting discussion of how Keaton's personal psychology may be involved in the film, see Judith Sanders and Daniel Lieberfeld, "Dreaming in Pictures: The Childhood Origins of Buster Keaton's Creativity," *Film Quarterly* 47:4 (Summer 1994): 14–28, esp. 21–3.
18. Stewart, "Keaton Through the Looking-Glass," p. 355.
19. Although some of the shots were done with the motorcycle fastened to a tracking car, others clearly show Keaton balancing and steering the motorcycle from the handlebars. "I got some beautiful spills," he remarked later, "some real beauties. I parked right on top of an automobile once. I hit it head on. I ended up with my fanny up against the windshield, my feet straight in the air" (Kevin Brownlow, *The Parade's Gone By* . . . [New York: Knopf, 1968], p. 314).
20. Moews, *Keaton: The Silent Features*, p. 79.

21. Stewart, "Keaton Through the Looking-Glass," p. 360.
22. Blesh, *Keaton,* pp. 151–2.
23. Stewart, "Keaton Through the Looking-Glass," p. 358.
24. Kerr, *The Silent Clowns,* p. 232.
25. Benjamin Lehmann, "Comedy and Laughter," in *Comedy: Meaning and Form,* ed. Robert W. Corrigan (Scranton, PA: Chandler, 1965), pp. 163–78.
26. Moews, *Keaton: The Silent Features,* p. 99.

3 The Detective and the Fool

OR, THE MYSTERY OF MANHOOD IN *SHERLOCK JR.*

One way or another, it appears, we all need a detective. Whether he is a private eye or a third ear, we need him to help us get our lives and their stories straight.

(Steven Marcus, *Freud and the Culture of Psychoanalysis*)[1]

[Sherlock Holmes was] one of the truly great comic characters in our literature . . . the classic caricature of the Amateur Detective in whose person the whole art of detection is made ridiculous. . . . [This is] what makes Holmes lovable and immortal.

(Christopher Isherwood, *Exhumations*)[2]

Buster Keaton's *Sherlock Jr.* – a film based on a figure famed for his ability to solve mysteries – ends with a little mystery of its own. After the crime has been solved and the "girl in the case" won, the hero, a young film projectionist and would-be private eye, embraces and then kisses his sweetheart while nervously but steadily taking his cues from the action on the screen before him. The kiss simultaneously indicates the formation of the heterosexual couple and the resolution of narrative conflict, and it is a convention in both dramatic comedy and Hollywood film overall. But when the film-within-a-film refuses to end as expected and continues with an image of the family life – including infant twins – that logically follows courtship, Sherlock Jr. pauses and scratches his head, ending the film on a note of ambiguity and leaving the viewer to ponder what gives him pause, what causes his paralysis before the specter of domestic life with the woman of his dreams. Is he wondering how babies are made – or if he wants any part of what goes along with making them?[3]

The answer might be found by examining *Sherlock Jr.* in the context of Keaton's other works, for it has much in common with them both structurally and thematically. Keaton often plays an adolescent boy on the brink of adulthood, staring ahead with uncertainty at the prospects of adult heterosexual love. In *Seven Chances* the hero is pursued by multitudes of overpowering women; in *Cops* rejection by his sweetheart causes him to choose jail over freedom; and in *College* the romance ends with an even more unsettling postscript, an image of a pair of tombstones over the dead couple.[4] A more promising clue, however, can be found in *Sherlock Jr.* itself – in particular, in its allusion to Sherlock Holmes, the fictional detective created by Arthur Conan Doyle around the turn of the century and enormously popular at the time Keaton made the film. What is the significance of the fact that the boy's fantasies, both waking and asleep, center on the great detective from Baker Street? When the young protagonist falls asleep and steps out of his boy body to become the man of his dreams, why is that man Holmes? The answer, I believe, illuminates not only *Sherlock Jr.* but our responses as gendered spectators to comedy in general.

In one of the first major feminist studies of film and one of the few to date to discuss the relation between gender and silent comedy, Molly Haskell asked in 1974 why the tradition of silent comedy seems to have had less appeal for women than for men. The answer, she suggested, lies in the fact that "most comedy is

FIGURE 11
Buster's movie theater boss catches him reading *How to Be a Detective* rather than doing his job as a cinema projectionist-janitor. *Sherlock Jr.* (Courtesy of KINO Video, New York.)

masculine" and that "ambivalence toward women, if not misogyny, was practically the stock in trade of silent comedy."[5] If overstated, Haskell's assessment still rings quite true. The canon of silent comedy is filled almost entirely with male directors and stars, who performed in modes – acrobatics, athletics, the physical aggression of slapstick – inconsistent with long-standing cultural ideals of femininity. And the films indeed seem to license an often startling degree of male infantilism and misogyny. Nonetheless, Haskell fails to acknowledge the pleasure comedies such as *Sherlock Jr.* provide for female viewers or the complexity of their appeal to men.

Narrative comedy is often described as a genre of wish fulfillment, siding with the forces of freedom (the young and the
powerless) as opposed to those of authority (the old and the
powerful) and working its thematic content out through a plot
that moves toward the union of a heterosexual couple. Even
comedian comedy such as Chaplin's and Keaton's, which places
greater emphasis on performance than on narrative, usually includes a romantic plot line.[6] This is true of *Sherlock Jr.*, in which
the young hero defeats his more powerful rival for the girl and
the couple's embrace, tentative though it may be, signals the
film's resolution. Of course, it is also important to keep in mind
whose fantasies comedy enacts and whose wishes it fulfills. In
general, the hero – especially in silent comedy – is most often
figured as a *male* youth, limiting the representational space available for women, if not for femininity, and this too is true of
Sherlock Jr., which beginning with its very title centers on a single
male who serves simultaneously as director and central character
of the movie. At the same time, however, the forces of authority
that comedy ridicules and defeats are also usually associated
with men, and so the genre is uniquely available for scrutinizing,
challenging, and correcting through laughter the abuses of masculinity as it is constructed in our culture. Moreover, because
viewers so readily dismiss comedy as "not serious," it provides a
safe place for engaging with models or figurations of masculinity
outside the norm. Such is the case with *Sherlock Jr.*, which follows
its young hero as he investigates not only a petty crime involving a stolen watch but the mysteries of adult sexuality and gender. In its exposure of the social construction of gender and its
ambivalence about the virtues of adult masculinity lie the film's
feminist interest and, I believe, appeal.

Now let us consider an episode in the film when, just before
the final chase, the hero escapes from his enemies by taking two
astonishing leaps. First, he vaults through a strange hoop or
circular case he has planted in a window and lands wearing a
dress. After discarding the disguise, he escapes yet again when
he sees his assistant, Gillette, the Watson figure, now disguised

as a woman. If we have missed the feminine imagery of the first leap, it is unmistakable in the second. In an even more spectacular cinematic trick, Sherlock Jr. plunges through Gillette's "belly" and disappears from pursuers and viewers alike until he can safely emerge on the other side of a swinging fence door, ready for the final pursuit that will hurl him out of his dream and into the waking reality he ultimately confronts in the film's final moments.

Over in a flash, these cinematic gags may be less celebrated than either *Sherlock Jr.*'s ambiguous ending or the virtuoso sequence in which the dreaming hero enters the film he is projecting. Yet they linger, resonating with the dream sequence that has long been understood as a key to the film. Whereas the dream only implies the relation between cinema and the unconscious, however, this sequence makes nearly *literal* the connection between a journey to the unconscious and a return to the womb. And in a film about the necessity of "reading" the world correctly, it begs a nod to Freud, another great detective and master of interpreting hidden signs. Uncannily, *Sherlock Jr.* brings together three phenomena born around the turn of the century: cinema, psychoanalysis, and the detective hero, and indeed Holmes's significance as the boy's ego ideal cannot fully be appreciated apart from Freud.

Much has already been written about *Sherlock Jr.*'s reflexivity and play with the relation between cinema, dream, and reality; and film theory has long explored the connection between the experience of watching a film and that of dreaming. Of all the cultural forces that shape our identities and fuel our desires, perhaps none is more seductive than the "dream machine" of cinema, which works its magic not only on the screen but through movie posters, fan magazines, and the entire apparatus of the institution. Feminist film theory in particular has studied the screen as a site for the projection of male fantasies or the desire of a patriarchal unconscious. In *Sherlock Jr.,* Keaton uses Holmes to evoke a particular kind of masculine fantasy, or fantasy about masculinity, that derives its authority from a claim to knowledge and the exercise of reason. Yet that knowledge reaches its limits at the threshold of sexual difference. Women remain for Holmes a disturbing threat to his authority and reminder of the limits of his power. And so Sherlock Jr. pauses in the final moments of the film before his long-sought prize.

At the same time, however, the detective is a figure well suited for holding that very model up to laughter, if not critique. Moving between crime and law, chaos and order, he stands as a figure of liminality, deriving his power from his contact with the margins and boundaries of our culture. As such, he is kin to another figure more fluid, more feminine, and more available to male and female viewers alike – the Fool – and in Keaton's hands he becomes just that. By invoking this tradition, Keaton's film opens up complex possibilities of identification: for female viewers, to appreciate the feminized male and, for male viewers, to engage in – and then disavow – the feminine within.

THE CRIME-CRUSHING CRIMINOLOGIST

Keaton made *Sherlock Jr.* during the heyday of what might be considered the "classical detective," a figure that flourished between 1887 and 1927, when Arthur Conan Doyle wrote the sixty narratives (four full-length novels and fifty-six short stories) that constitute the Holmes saga. That saga has since been enriched by an enormous body of Sherlockiana (work on Holmes, not his creator), which testifies to the detective's enduring appeal and includes more than three hundred films.[7] Holmes's cultural impact is suggested, as one critic has noted, by "the belief held for years by thousands, that he was an actual living human being – a circumstance that constitutes one of the most unusual chapters in literary history."[8]

Holmes's literary roots can be traced to the writings in the 1840s of Edgar Allen Poe, who is often credited with having originated both the short story and the detective genre, a form of fiction that anticipated Holmes's eventual incarnation in film by helping to pave the way for mass culture.[9] After Poe's detective, Dupin, came similar character types, including Holmes, Agatha Christie's Hercule Poirot, and a series of more "hard-boiled" detectives beginning in the 1920s – the tough private investigators of Dashiell Hammett, Raymond Chandler, and Ross McDonald. Most recently, writers such as Sarah Paretsky, Sue Grafton, Linda Barnes, and Patricia Cornwell have added female investigators, and feminist perspectives, to the tradition.[10]

While the character of Holmes is associated with crime, the books and films about him depict little actual violence, suggesting that the real nature of his appeal lies elsewhere. Most obviously, it concerns the apparent power of the mind to reduce the world and its mysteries to explanations that are "logical" and to connections that are "elementary." Yet as one critic has observed, "The Sherlockian mode of procedure, although labelled as deductive and logical, is really intuitive and illogical," more an exercise of imagination and bricolage than of formal analysis.[11] This would suggest that the detective serves a cultural function related less to logic itself than to the *myth* of logic, and less to science and reason than to the need for a belief, or *faith,* in science and reason.

According to Sigfried Kracauer, fiction based on the classical detective can arise only within traditions of liberal democracy or, as Thomas Schatz suggests, in societies that understand the universe as benevolent and crime as individual and isolated, not social. In such a universe, the detective's superior mind enables him to quickly locate individual guilt and restore social order. The detective is "the predestined hero of a civilized world which believes in the blessings of enlightenment and individual freedom, . . . the single-handed sleuth who makes reason destroy the spider webs of irrational powers and decency triumph over dark instincts."[12] "Highly cultured, aristocratic, eccentric, scientific, . . . capable of complex deductive reasoning" and in possession of a "cultivated wit," he is typified in film by the performances of Basil Rathbone and John Barrymore as Holmes, Warner Oland as Charlie Chan, Peter Lorre as Mr. Moto, and William Powell as the Thin Man.[13]

While the shift in the 1920s from the classical detective to the tough private investigator signaled a declining faith in liberalism, the genre betrayed a sense of cultural malaise from the outset with its tone of nostalgia, evident in *Sherlock Jr.*'s Victorian setting. As Franco Moretti explains, the detective represents the panoptical eye of late capitalism, providing a means of policing – like mass culture itself – more effective than the formal institutions designated to do so. Superior to the bungling investigators of Scotland Yard, Holmes controls by "seeing" the secrets of those who take refuge in private spaces. By linking crime with isolation and the criminal with social upstarts committed to "risky and excessive individualism" in their own self-interest, detective fiction enabled the middle class to identify itself with "prudence and stasis."[14] And so in *Sherlock Jr.*, the sheik, who courts the girl not for love but to further his own greedy and lustful desires, represents the social bounder as criminal.

It is not Holmes, however, but Freud, another physician-writer like Doyle, who might well be considered the consummate investigator of late-Victorian and early-twentieth-century culture and the key to Holmes's significance as a model of masculinity. Like Holmes, Freud created a new analytical method to explain a reality that no longer made sense, and like Holmes, his impact has been greater in the realm of myth than in that of science. While both Holmes and Freud served as social healers delivering their societies from guilt and providing a method of mastery over forces that seemed beyond individual control, the detective story flourished at a moment in history when, as Steven Marcus has noted, the locus of mystery began to shift from the exterior world Holmes explores to the interior one of Freud.[15] For Freud, the greatest mystery is human identity, driven by the unconscious; the most gripping crime drama, located in the family and configured by the Oedipal triangle, and the most compelling criminal, the Father.

Sherlock Jr. is organized around two worlds, and two quests, that turn in parallel ways on the boy's relationship with the Father, or his exploration of adult masculinity. In the opening moments of the film, we meet the protagonist and learn of his desire to be a detective. However, like Johnny Gray, who will follow in *The General* (1926/7) and who loves only his engine and Annabelle, he has another desire as well, and that is for "the girl in the case." The two desires appear to be bound to one another and to the issue of sexual maturity: the boy, it would seem, cannot win the girl (one of the rewards of adult masculinity) without first proving himself as a detective and gaining the invulnerability and power of the adult male. Until – or unless – he does, he remains female-identified and feminized, inhabiting a dangerous world in which all adult men are his enemies. This linking of a male hero's quest in the public sphere with a reward – a woman – in the private sphere is an enduring narrative structure that occurs in most Hollywood films, and at this point in the film – although not later, as we have already seen – it appears inevitable and beyond question. And so the fake mustache the boy wears in the opening shots is not only a prop or disguise associated with detectives, but also an emblem of adult masculinity. His romantic rival, the sheik, wears a mustache, which gives his identity away at a crucial moment.

The use of the detective as a model for the hero signals from the outset that this is a film about clues and about the necessity of reading the world and its seemingly trivial details as signs, full of meaning. Among the most important of these concern gender, which the film shows to be a product of social codes, something to be studied and absorbed from the symbolic systems – such as those found in popular fiction and, more dramatically, cinema – that channel our desires and dreams into culturally appropriate directions. Indeed, the film derives much of its comedy from its satire of the infatuation of adolescents with screen idols – whether Mary Pickford, whose poster hangs in the theater lobby, or Rudolph Valentino, the model for the sheik, or John Barrymore, who played Holmes in a film two years before *Sherlock Jr.*[16] And so the fake mustache suggests not only adult masculinity but its *social construction* and the fact that gender itself is less a biological condition than a social role, even disguise, that can be acquired by studying the clues and manuals our culture provides. Not only is femininity a masquerade, as has so often been argued in feminist film studies and psychoanalysis, but masculinity is as well, capable of being put on or taken off at will like the false mustache that reappears at crucial moments in the film.

Many of these signs are indicated as such by the film's use of frames and the motif of framing, which replicate its thematic concern with the "framing" of the hero and heroine in social codes that shape their identities as male and female. Movie posters and sports photographs depict iconic images of femininity and masculinity, and mirrors, windows, doors, the theater's proscenium arch and projection booth regularly set off images of the boy and girl performing their respective roles. The film's plot depends on the hero's being "framed" by his rival for a crime he did not commit. Most important, Keaton structures the plot with a frame story, embedding the hero's dream-entry into *Hearts and Pearls,* the film he is projecting, in a parallel "real-world" story.

Set in the Victorian Age, the frame story draws on that era's strict definitions of gender to map out the Oedipal conflict that drives the film's narrative. Associated with pre-Oedipal sexuality, the young protagonist is Sherlock Jr., and standing between him and his desires are a host of "bad fathers" – at best weak, at worst dangerous. Here authority and power reside in the hands of fathers who rule through muscle or brute force, leaving the boy – like women and weaker men – vulnerable, in effect feminized. In the theater, his boss scolds him for reading his detective manual, hands him a broom, and kicks him. A huge bully threatens him, then takes a wallet full of money from the pile of trash he was sweeping up. The girl's father, while well intentioned, is easily duped. The first extended gag of the film, about the lost dollar, turns on the boy's "housecleaning," or performing women's work.

Most menacing of all is Sherlock Jr.'s rival, the sheik, and the film emphasizes the discrepancy in their sizes with the vaudeville turn in which the boy shadows him. When Sherlock Jr. offers the girl a token of his love appropriate to his own size (a ring with a stone she cannot see), he wishes to present himself as "bigger" than he is by giving her an expensive box of candy. The sheik doesn't have money either, but he doesn't hesitate to steal it and offer the girl the bigger box of candy. And later, it is not only his mustache but his size that gives the sheik away. The sheik humiliates the boy with his offer of a banana and the gag that follows. Even more devastatingly, he beats the aspiring detective at his own game. When he surveys the situation in the girl's house and sees the boy wooing her, he also sees an opportunity to beat the boy by stealing the watch. Later, when the boy takes out his manual on how to solve a crime, the sheik looks over his shoulder at the words "search everyone," interpreting that information as a clue about how to frame the detective himself. This world of threatening bad fathers and weak good ones is one in which not only women and children, but men as well, have much to fear. To find his way out of it, the boy turns to the model of the detective.

THE DREAM, OR THE FANTASY OF THE PHALLUS

When the boy steps out of his sleeping body to enter the film he is projecting, he also enters a fantasy of life on the other side of the Oedipal passage, beyond the frustrated desires of adolescence. Here he succeeds in defeating the sheik, or "bad father," and taking on the identity of Holmes, the "good father," who possesses all the mastery promised to the boy on his arrival at maturity. Yet he achieves that mastery not through the brute force that overpowered him in the frame story, but through something he would like to see as both more powerful and more available to him. Holmes asserts the superiority of reason over the forces of the material world, and of "class" over crudeness. In the dream, it doesn't matter that he is small and weak; his mastery of abstraction enables him to defeat the bullies who blocked his desire in the frame story. If, in Lacanian terms, the frame story depicts the boy in the world of the penis, the dream represents the triumph of the Phallus or the Symbolic.

That triumph is also accompanied by rupture and division, however, and as the sleeping boy gives parthenogenic birth to Sherlock Jr. a double exposure holds the two figures in the same frame. And so the dream not only reworks the events of the frame story but intensifies them. The stakes become higher, and the danger greater. The setting has shifted from a Victorian past to the contemporary Jazz Age. The girl in the case is no longer a child-woman but a sophisticated flapper. Like Holmes, the sheik now wears a tuxedo, and he comes with a gang of henchmen who threaten the hero with bombs, axes, poison, and even death by imprisonment in a hanging cage, one of the most bizarre images of framing or confinement in the film. Now the sheik doesn't steal the father's watch, an object distant from the girl, but her pearls, and to steal her pearls comes close to stealing her heart. And now Sherlock Jr. isn't driven to save the girl only from the threat of losing her to a rival, but from kidnapping and the threat of rape.

But the dream reverses the dynamics of the frame story. Whereas the boy was incompetent and foolish, now the fathers are the clowns. Sherlock Jr. intimidates his opponents when he first meets them, outwits them in the pool game, and repeatedly escapes their traps. Whereas the sheik represents a limited kind of masculine power based on the physical force called up by the images of boxers on the hideout wall, Holmes represents something quite different. Alluding not only to the character Doyle created in fiction but to the one John Barrymore created in film two years earlier, Holmes provides a cultivated and aristocratic image of masculine power associated with the high art of the stage rather than the more lowly screen. As an investigator he acquires power not by physically overpowering his enemies but through the more abstract form of knowledge. Now he examines the world through his ever-present magnifying glass and watches his suspects in the mirror, reading their behavior for clues about what to do. Over and over he escapes catastrophe, and even if most often it's only by chance, that only enhances the sense of entitlement and invulnerability about him.

Male heroes are traditionally tested by quests that require them to journey across landscapes, often figured as feminine, and in his dream Sherlock Jr. becomes a hero by demonstrating his mastery of physical space. When he first tries to enter the film, he finds himself in a world that, through editing, metamorphoses around him at every turn. He does not "fit" or belong. Yet by the end of the dream he does, and he shows himself not mastered by but master *of* space, his small body now heroic. In the final chase he again travels across a vast landscape that changes before our eyes, but now he is not edited out; rather, he is integrated in, his physical prowess displayed in long takes and deep-space compositions. Perched on the handlebars of a driverless motorcycle, he rides gloriously to his destination, penetrating crowds of people, barging through barriers, leaving wreckage behind him but himself remaining untouched. The world rearranges itself according to his needs – a pair of trucks converge to provide him a bridge, vehicles assume unworldly shapes to allow him to move through them unharmed.

Even more suggestively, Sherlock Jr. displays a mastery of the symbolic systems of our culture, not only by entering the film he projects but by altering it according to his desire. *Hearts and Pearls or the Lounge Lizard's Lost Love* is a melodrama or "woman's film," which Keaton gently satirizes by naming its producer (Veronal Film Co.) after a sedative and having the film put even the feminized hero to sleep.[17] Once Sherlock Jr. enters the melodrama, it takes on the distinctly more masculine flavor of an action adventure film.

Throughout the dream, the film plays with the motif of metamorphosis, which also recalls the disguises of the fictional Holmes. If we witness changes in landscape and genre, however, those changes are only backdrops for the crucial change the dream explores, the boy's transformation into a man. That transformation culminates in the sequence I described at the beginning of this essay, when, just before that final ride but after he has reclaimed the pearls, the hero escapes by plunging first through the circular case and then through the "woman's" belly. At this moment it is clear that he cannot escape danger or fulfill his desires without first returning to the original site of danger and desire. Here he successfully navigates the Oedipal passage, returning to the mother's womb, then putting that original object of desire aside to emerge a man. Moments later, after his miraculous disappearance, we see that new man clinging safely on the other side of the fence, reborn into adulthood.[18]

THE "GIRL IN THE CASE," OR THE CASE OF THE MISSING GIRL

Meanwhile, where does all this leave the girl? For, along with her pearls, she has disappeared from the film-within-a-film. Here *Sherlock Jr.* begins to suggest the meaning of adult heterosexuality for women, and that meaning – not surprisingly – is quite different from what it is for men. The girl's transformation into a woman also moves her forward into the Jazz Age, a setting that would appear to offer her greater freedom as a woman. Yet that apparent advance is as illusory as the dream itself. If adult heterosexuality liberates the boy, it does just the opposite for the girl. The dream removes her from any agency or even presence in the film, rendering her at best a structural absence.

Initially, in the frame story, she seems confined both to a subordinate position in the narrative and to a highly constricted notion of Victorian femininity – sentimentalized, childlike, asexual, like the poster of Mary Pickford ("America's Sweetheart") that hangs in the theater lobby. Masculinity is something the boy learns through active study, a dynamic and conflict-ridden business that provides the narrative and comic momentum of the film. In contrast, femininity appears to be a timeless state of being, something the girl inhabits unconsciously and absorbs passively from the images the culture provides. The film introduces the boy engaged in activity at his place of work; it introduces her posed in a Victorian pinup, kneeling in a pastoral setting, feeding a large pet dog. Like the boy, she is universalized by having no name, but her story is subordinated to his. With the exception of her dream counterpart, there is only one female character in the film, only one model of femininity available to her, and only one position for her in the narrative – to be "the girl in the case," the sweetheart, the reward that motivates Sherlock Jr.[19]

However, if the pre-Oedipal world is one from which the boy has good reason to wish to escape, that is not the case for the girl. The film's visual compositions in the frame story convey an equality between male and female. Especially in the courtship sequence, symmetrically composed shots emphasize the similarities between the boy and girl in movement and size. When the boy gives her the ring with the nearly invisible stone and then attempts to hold her hand, an extended take shows them in a two-shot seated side by side on a sofa. Even more dramatically, the film's overall narrative structure tips the balance in favor of the girl, whose actions and their effects significantly undercut the boy's eventual heroics. While the overall effect of the courting sequence conveys the excruciating self-consciousness of adolescence, especially in this reconstruction of the Victorian Age, the girl's actions belie the myth of woman as girl, and girl as passive and asexual. She takes the initiative sexually, losing patience with the boy's shyness and grabbing hold of his hand. Most strikingly, it is she who solves the crime, acting logically and effectively to clear the boy's name and outwit *both* of her suitors. In effect, along with the femininity she inhabits so unconsciously, she also possesses those masculine powers that the boy is laboring so tediously to acquire. But while the boy suffers from his feminization, she enjoys the mastery that is offered to the boy in the end.

Her mastery is short-lived, however, for as the dream advances the couple into heterosexual maturity, we learn the social meaning of femininity as well as masculinity. The hero's authority comes at the cost of hers; his role is to be active and dominant, hers to be passive and submissive. Initially the flapper presents a more interesting image on the screen, a relief, even, after the cloying sweetness of the girl. However, that sexual charge serves only to make her a more desirable prize for the boy. In the boy's dream, as opposed to the frame story, the girl does not take matters into her own hands to solve the crime, but becomes a crime victim herself – robbed, assaulted, abducted. The threat of rape increases the drama of the boy's maniacal ride to the rescue, and her vulnerability only enhances his heroism. In effect, she is erased from the action of the film, and hardly missed.

Indeed, the boy's story – and the cinematic pleasure of Keaton's athletic, space-devouring performance – demand her absence, for the boy cannot blossom as man and Keaton as a comedian until she disappears. We see her only long enough at the beginning of the dream to place her in the plot; she and her pearls provide a motive for the investigation that will allow Sherlock Jr. to prove his valor as a detective. Then she vanishes while Sherlock Jr. moves through a series of extended gags in his attempt to find the missing pearls. She does not reappear until the end when she is reintroduced to heighten the temporal pressure on the hero during the final chase. Because the distance or unattainability of the love object fuels romantic desire, the fate of the dream heroine suggests how a woman's absence and vulnerability only enhance her desirability.

When assessing the importance of the girl's solving the case, it is important to consider when and how that information is conveyed to us. Keaton might well have withheld it until after the dream, but he did not. By letting us in on this information before the dream occurs – in effect, by framing the dream with it – Keaton shifts the focus of narrative suspense from the enigmas posed in the frame story to a different set of issues. Not having to worry about whether the boy will clear himself of a false accusation and reclaim his sweetheart, we can now turn our attention to how well he will navigate himself through an ever-escalating series of tests. It is no longer the boy's future with the girl that is at stake – but his present, *with the boys.*

This desire to take on the power and freedom of adulthood without the demands represented by women and domestic responsibilities is further suggested by the two models of masculinity Keaton holds up for examination – the sheik and the detective; and a comparison between them shows why Sherlock Jr.'s retreat from his prize at the end is inevitable. Typically in a comedy with a romantic triangle, the young male hero faces an older rival who is socially more powerful but sexually less so; and comedy invariably sides with youth and freedom as opposed to age, authority, and law. *Sherlock Jr.,* however, inverts that familiar pattern. Here the rival – and villain – is explicitly more sexual than the boy's ego ideal and exudes the danger of masculine sexuality. He is a "lounge lizard," a gigolo, an implicit reference to Rudolph Valentino, the great male sex symbol of the 1920s who while often considered suspiciously feminine was associated above all with an irresistible sex appeal. The sheik aggressively courts the girl with a sense of sexual entitlement that contrasts with the boy's comically timid moves. In the dream he doesn't simply kiss the girl's hand, as he did in the frame story, but grabs her and kisses her aggressively, and again, it is his sexual move on the girl that causes the boy to spring frantically to action.

If the sheik's sleaziness and villainy cast an ambivalence around male sexuality, the character of the detective further complicates that ambivalence. In general, Holmes sublimates his sexuality in favor of the wider-reaching power of the Symbolic, or the Phallus. Still, the knowledge he obtains and his means of doing so are not entirely asexual in their implications. A detective enters forbidden spaces and has knowledge of mysterious business, including that most mysterious business of all, the passions and drives that originate in the unconscious. His technology of surveillance may be microscopic rather than telescopic, the magnifying glass rather than the more panoptical binoculars, yet their effect is the same, a reminder that detective work, like cinema, is a voyeuristic enterprise, a license to watch private activities unobserved and to penetrate the private lives of others, much as the sheik does in the doorway of the girl's house.[20] In the frame story, the boy searches the girl by timidly peeking into her pockets, and he himself becomes the victim of the sheik's intrusion on his body. In the dream, Sherlock Jr.'s first gesture on entering the house is to boldly "search every-body" by marching into the personal space of his suspects, including the girl, and peering intently at them.

Despite Sherlock Jr.'s apparent interest in the girl, Holmes is better known for an extreme misogyny. As Marcello Truzzi writes, "Holmes's skepticism of appearances bordered upon the paranoic when it came to women: Holmes was especially cautious in his relations with women and found it nearly impossible to correctly assess their motives."[21] That misogyny is consistent with the tradition of "terminal bachelorhood" Kenneth Calhoon has noted among the legendary detectives, from Sherlock Holmes to Hercule Poirot and Father Brown, and it might in fact be understood as motivating his very investigative method. Because pathos threatens logos, the boundary between them must be rigorously guarded. And because women excite the passions and threaten the source of the detective's power, they represent a kind of taboo.[22]

This antipathy toward women has sometimes been interpreted as homosexual in origin, and indeed Holmes's most intimate relationship is with Watson, another man. In describing the totalitarian impulses of the detective novel, Moretti cites a passage from "A Case of Identity" which also suggests that intimacy: " 'My dear fellow,' says Holmes to Watson, 'if we could fly out that great window hand in hand, hover over this great city, gently remove the roofs, and peep in at the queer things which are going on. . . .' "[23] The gendered relationships of the Holmesian universe might more accurately be explained, however, by the structure of desire Eve Sedgwick has described as homosocial, a term used in history and the social sciences to describe social bonds among people of the same sex. Her argument begins with the work of René Girard, who suggested that in the romantic triangle of two men and a woman (e.g., the boy, the sheik, and the girl), the real play of desire is often not male to female, but male to male.[24] This desire may or may not be be overtly sexual but it does involve eros of another kind – the drive to identify with and emulate an admired other. The Oedipal struggle between father and son is thus infused not only with enmity but with admiration and love, which explains in part the intensity of the struggle and the complexity of the bonds between the two.

Yet those bonds exist within a logic of sameness rather than difference, a logic that, as Sedgwick explains, functions historically and politically as a kind of "social glue" that fosters the maintenance and transferral of power in patriarchal society. Homosociality encompasses "male friendship, mentorship, entitlement, rivalry, and hetero- and homosexuality,"[25] attachments that link men together along a continuum of desire between homosocial and homosexual. This structure allows for hierarchy without difference, and it explains the relationships between men so familiar in Western literature and culture, beginning with the Socratic dialogues and including not only Watson's relationship with Holmes but the boy's with his fictional ideal. Watson occupies the place of a woman in a servant–master relationship with Holmes, his obtuseness allowing Holmes to demonstrate his own greater powers of reason.

And so the boy's dream might finally be understood as driven less by heterosexual desire for the girl than by homosocial desire for a boys-only club where no girls are allowed, a fantasy that combines the heightened drama and excitement of the action adventure film with the comfort of the buddy film. Thus, the dream re-creates a less sinister version of what Pleasure Island offered Pinocchio, or Never-Never Land offered Peter Pan and the Lost Boys, a space where they will never grow up and can always play with Pirates and Indians because Wendy remains in the background to mother them and Tinkerbell is only a tiny sprite.

Sherlock Jr. begins with the hero seeking to satisfy two desires: to be a detective and to get the girl. As I mentioned earlier, these desires appear fundamentally connected. By the end, he has tried on the identity of the detective / adult male, and in his dream, if not in the frame story, he has solved the crime and proved himself. But when offered the prize, he balks. Perhaps, the film suggests, the real reward of manhood is the freedom to do away with women altogether.

FEMINISM AND COMEDY, OR THE DETECTIVE AS FOOL

All of this might suggest that Haskell's assessment is correct. Despite the power Keaton gives the girl in the frame story – and often the female leads of his other films – that power is easily forgotten in the boy's ambivalence toward her and in the sheer cinematic and comedic pleasure of watching his dream unfold without her. Yet it is important not to discount a fundamental element of this film – in fact, its most fundamental element: Keaton's transformation of the great detective into a Fool and what gets altered as well in the process.

Holmes was already ripe for parody by the time *Sherlock Jr.* was filmed, and Keaton was not the first filmmaker to exploit that comic potential. Indeed, a number of spoofs had already appeared as early as 1911, including *The Two Sleuths* series produced by Mack Sennett (D. W. Griffith directed *Trailing the Counterfeiters*), another series called *Sherlocko and Watso,* and mysteries that mocked the detective's name (*Suelock Jones, Detective* and *Sherlock Bonehead*).[26] As one critic has suggested, what Holmes describes as "absurdly simple" might better be described as "simply absurd," and others have referred less ambiguously to the "cataract of drivel for which Conan Doyle is responsible" and described Sherlock Holmes as an "inspired imbecile."[27] The ease of Keaton's transformation of Holmes from a sober figure of male power into the subject of (male and female) laughter arises not only from the figure's potential absurdity, however, but from something else he shares with the traditional figure of the Fool – and that is his association with cultural margins and his identity as a boundary crosser.

Human culture depends on the creation of conceptual categories that are upheld by demarcating the boundaries between them – categories that distinguish between, for example, male and female, inside and out, finite and infinite, body and spirit. Certain figures, such as priests and shamans, serve as mediators between these categories, crossing the boundaries between them and moving from one to another. As Calhoon has suggested, Victorian society projected onto the criminal all that seemed "excessively human," all those traces of the body, materiality, and contingency that it wished to cast off and conceal from itself.[28] And so the detective – who could read those traces – became a figure of mediation, moving between a bourgeois society governed by law and a criminal world out of reach, excessive, extraordinary. Indeed, if the detective is bound to any human being, it is neither to a woman nor even his male partner but to the criminal he pursues (in *Sherlock Jr.*, the sheik). This contact with taboo contributes to the element of the demonic already implied by Holmes's metamorphosis through the use of disguises. It also further explains his celibacy, which marks him as an outsider, never fully able to participate in ordinary social life but possessing power beyond it.[29]

Similarly the Fool, a figure from literary and social history, resides on the margins of society. Yet whereas the detective is deadly earnest, if cynical, about the world he investigates and protects, the Fool mocks it and its pretensions. Whereas the detective soberly defends the foundations of society – including, as we have seen, the primacy of logos over pathos, male over female – the Fool opposes all that the social world deems serious. And while usually male like the classical detective, the Fool is often androgynous or hermaphroditic, encompassing both male and female traits.[30] Like the detective, the Fool exists apart from marriage, the foundation of kinship systems and social order. But unlike the detective, he acts to destabilize rather than uphold the hierarchies on which that order rests. This tradition underlies Keaton's persona, and the Fool's mask is etched on his beautiful face, just as it later appears in the characters created by Samuel Beckett, who was inspired by Keaton in creating his own absurd universe.

The Fool gives yet another perspective on the boy of the frame story, whose ambivalence about the girl might also be read as an affirmation of pre-Oedipal identity, with its fluid and unstable boundaries between male and female, inside and out, adult and child. Perhaps the final gesture of the film might be interpreted not only as a disavowal of the responsibilities of adult heterosexuality, but also as a refusal of its social asymmetries, an acceptance of the fact that women cannot be permanently written out of the plot, because the passage of time ultimately undoes us all. And so if on one level *Sherlock Jr.* seems to endorse a rejection of women and the domestic, on another level it renders *all* social roles suspect, especially those tied to the legitimate authority of the "fathers." *Sherlock Jr.* casts a skeptical eye on adult masculinity, whether figured as the sheik or as Sherlock Holmes, and indeed, comedy – the genre in which Keaton chose to work – provides one of the few spaces where masculinity can be safely held up for ridicule and men not taken seriously.

This accounts for an intriguing difference between Keaton and many other performers in the tradition of comedian comedy. Unlike the Three Stooges or Jerry Lewis, for example, Keaton's persona conveys intelligence rather than stupidity, and a sincere – if comical – struggle with the demands placed on him as a man, rather than self-indulgence.[31] Even more to the point, he avoids – at least in *Sherlock Jr.* – the blatant targeting of women as phallic figures of repression, or dowager killjoys, that is common in U.S. popular culture and especially in comedian comedy. Such a targeting displaces the anger comedy mobilizes against pretense and repression from its rightful sources – those who hold power in our culture – to others less deserving of it. This displacement surely contributes to the antipathy that, as Molly Haskell has argued, many women feel toward silent comedy, for the spectacle of men acting like babies and throwing tantrums at powerful bad mothers must undoubtedly elicit different reactions from women than from men. In *The Fool and His Scepter*, William Willeford describes the Fool as mother-bound, identified with women because, like women, he is removed from the center of social power and subject to the authority of the King. Likewise in *Sherlock Jr.*, Keaton holds the father, not the mother, responsible for opposing the wishes of the protagonist and the values of liberation that comedy so often affirms.

This identification with the feminine suggests yet another explanation for the pleasure comedy such as Keaton's provides both male and female viewers – a pleasure that may arise less out of any specific critique of masculinity than out of the more subtle processes of identification and disavowal Freud explained in *The Interpretation of Dreams*. Like Chaplin, Keaton as a performer was coded as feminine, and indeed he made an arresting "woman" when he performed in drag, as in *The Play House*. Perhaps the Fool or the "little guy" provides men with a sympathetic figure that enables them to recognize the femininity they are encouraged to repress in themselves – then disavow it because it appears in the "unserious" form of comedy. And he offers women a rare image of male defensiveness, incompetence, and foolishness. As Julia Lesage suggests, women may be raised to desire "real men," or what the culture designates as "real" masculinity, but they can also appreciate representations of men (not to mention men themselves) that deviate significantly from that ideal.[32] Keaton's detective-as-fool reminds both men and women of the unattainability and *undesirability* of "real manhood" as it is embodied by the detective-as-hero.

Here I would like to return to the idea of melodrama briefly mentioned earlier. Keaton is known for his interest in melodrama, and I believe that interest accounts for the melancholy so often associated with his work. Indeed, *Our Hospitality* is a good example of how deeply Keaton is willing to venture into melodrama before reversing himself, and of how powerfully melodrama then colors the rest of the film. *Sherlock Jr.* mocks melodrama not only with the joke about its sedating effect on men, but with the transformation of *Hearts and Pearls* in the dreaming mind of Keaton's projectionist, thus creating a film-within-the-film. Yet it is not *Hearts and Pearls* but the frame story in which the film's melodrama lies, in which both the the girl and the boy are victims of a repressive gender system and the social order it upholds. Here Keaton exposes the abuses that arise from this order, yet that exposure never becomes self-pitying, because it is ironized, framed from the outset in comedy. As the Fool, Keaton invites our laughter not only at the adult men who victimize him but at his own desire to share their power, to become Sherlock Sr.

Keaton's "Fool-ishness" is possible, of course, only because of his brilliance as a performer and director, and the film is above all a vehicle for displaying his very real mastery of the language of cinema and comedy. Yet he *does* play the Fool, and with every blunder and pratfall he makes us laugh not only at the gap between the Sherlock Holmes of legend and Sherlock Jr., but also at the very aspirations toward mastery embodied in the mythic detective. In so doing, he creates a space for mocking a heroic ideal of masculinity, exposing its lunacy, and suggesting its contribution to our culture's social ills. If the detective attempts to cure those ills through logic, then, and the psychoanalyst through listening, Keaton as Fool unsettles them through an uncanny but cathartic laughter.

NOTES

1. Quoted in Michael Shepherd, *Sherlock Holmes and the Case of Dr. Freud* (New York: Tavistock, 1985), p. 26.
2. Quoted in ibid., p. 20.
3. These questions are Andy Horton's, and I am grateful to him for his skills as an editor, his generosity as a host, and, above all, his insights into comedy. Thanks to Sean Axmaker for sharing his

Hong Kong laser disc copy of *Sherlock Jr.* and to Linda Kintz and Julia Lesage for helpful comments on earlier drafts of this essay. Thanks also to the other contributors to this volume, who provided helpful information and congenial companionship during a working session in New Orleans.

4. An auteurist approach would note the similarities between *Sherlock Jr.* and Keaton's other films. In addition to endings that undercut the heterosexual couple, these include episodes in which the hero falls asleep, dream sequences, instances of divided or multiple selves, and structures that establish the hero's incompetence in the first half followed by his competence in the second. For discussions of these similarities, see David Robinson, *Buster Keaton* (London: Secker & Warbury, 1970); Daniel Moews, *Keaton: The Silent Features Close Up* (Berkeley: University of California Press, 1977); and Gilberto Perez, "The Bewildered Equilibrist: An Essay on Buster Keaton's Comedy," *Hudson Review* 34:3 (1981): 337–66.

5. Molly Haskell, *From Reverence to Rape* (New York: Holt, Rinehart & Winston, 1974), p. 68. Since Haskell, Patricia Mellencamp and Lucy Fischer have written the most influential feminist work on film comedy (Lucy Fischer, "Sometimes I Feel Like a Motherless Child: Comedy and Matricide," in *Comedy/Cinema/Theory*, ed. Andrew Horton [Berkeley: University of California Press, 1991], pp. 60–78; Patricia Mellencamp, "Situation Comedy, Feminism and Freud: Discourses of Gracie and Lucy," in *Studies in Entertainment*, ed. Tania Modleski [Bloomington: Indiana University Press, 1986], pp. 80–95; idem, "Jokes and Their Relation to the Marx Brothers," in *Cinema and Language*, ed. Stephen Heath and Patricia Mellencamp [Frederick, MD: University Publications of America, 1986], pp. 63–78; and idem, *High Anxiety: Catastrophe, Scandal, Age & Comedy* [Bloomington: Indiana University Press, 1992]), but other feminist scholars are now publishing on the subject. See Kristine Brunovska Karnick, "Commitment and Reaffirmation in Hollywood Romantic Comedy," in *Classical Hollywood Comedy*, ed. Kristine Brunovska Karnick and Henry Jenkins (New York: Routledge, 1995), pp. 123–46; Tina Olsen Lent, "Romantic Love and Friendship: The Redefinition of Gender Relations in Screwball Comedy," in ibid., pp. 314–31; Ramona Curry, "*Goin' to Town* and Beyond: Mae West, Film Censorship and the Comedy of *Un*marriage," in ibid., pp. 211–37; Pamela Robertson, *Guilty Pleasures: Feminist Camp from Mae West to Madonna* (Durham, NC: Duke University Press, 1996); and idem, " 'The Kinda Comedy That Imitates Me': Mae West's Identification with the Feminist Camp," *Cinema Journal* 32:2 (1993): 57–72.

6. See Northrop Frye's classic analysis of the narrative structure of comedy, *Anatomy of Criticism: Four Essays* (Princeton, NJ: Princeton University Press, 1957). David Bordwell, Janet Staiger, and Kristin Thompson found that 95 out of 100 classical Hollywood films included a romantic subplot (*The Classical Hollywood Cinema: Film Style and Mode of Production to 1960* [New York: Columbia University Press, 1985]).

7. See Robert W. Pohle, Jr., and Douglas C. Hart, *Sherlock Holmes on the Screen: The Motion Picture Adventures of the World's Most Popular Detective* (South Brunswick, NJ: Barnes, 1977), for an overview of films based on Holmes. (Chris Steinbrunner and Norman Michaels, *The Films of Sherlock Holmes* [Secaucus, NJ: Citadel Press, 1978], also survey the field.) The earliest include American Mutograph and Biograph Company's *Sherlock Holmes Baffled* (1903, possibly as early as 1900) and Vitagraph's *Adventures of Sherlock Holmes* (in 1905, possibly 1903). See Shepherd's *Sherlock Holmes and the Case of Dr. Freud* for a discussion of the history of Sherlockiana, which has undoubtedly expanded to include fan groups on the Internet.

8. The passage is quoted in Marcello Truzzi, "Sherlock Holmes: Applied Social Psychologist," in *The Sign of Three: Dupin, Holmes, Peirce,* ed. Umberto Eco and Thomas A. Sebeok (Bloomington: Indiana University Press, 1983), pp. 55–80.

9. I am indebted to Franco Moretti's *Signs Taken for Wonders,* trans. Susan Fischer, David Forgaes, and David Miller (New York: Verso, 1983), for pointing out to me the connections between Holmes, psychoanalysis and late Victorian capitalism. Kenneth S. Calhoon's insightful and wide-ranging essay ("The Detective and the Witch: Local Knowledge in Conan Doyle and Fontane," *Comparative Literature* 47:4 [1995]: 307–29) has similarly influenced my thinking and directed me to Kracauer's writing on the detective. Calhoon draws on Kracauer's untranslated *Schriften,* Vol. 1, to argue that detective fiction helps define the modern sensibility in terms of a tension between interiority and "facades" or surfaces.

10. The works of these writers feature female characters who investigate crimes in a variety of professional and amateur capacities (as private eyes, a taxi driver, a coroner). Jill Churchill has written a series based on a housewife who is an amateur detective, and Barbara Neely has written about a black domestic. The impact of these writers has contributed to a greater awareness not only of gender issues but of race and class. My thanks to Nanci La Velle for this information.

11. The quotation (from Shepherd, *Sherlock Holmes and the Case of Dr. Freud*, p. 20) continues by contrasting the pleasure afforded by Holmes's method with the "tedium" of a "true analytic detective story." In "The Detective and the Witch," Calhoon writes that "despite his insistent invocation of 'logic,' Holmes does not express his understanding of the world in terms of formal relations, but through signs (clues in which concepts and perceptions coincide). This is the 'local knowledge' of the bricoleur" (p. 10).

12. Sigfried Kracauer, *From Caligari to Hitler* (Princeton, NJ: Princeton University Press, 1947), p. 20.

13. Thomas Schatz, *Hollywood Film Genres: Formulas, Filmmaking, and the Studio System* (New York: McGraw-Hill, 1981), p. 124.

14. Moretti, *Signs Taken for Wonders*, p. 139.

15. Marcus is quoted in Shepherd's discussion of the similarities between Freud and Holmes, including Freud's acknowledgment that he read Doyle seriously. In a letter to Jung, Freud said in reference to his work, "I made it appear as though the most tenuous of clues had enabled me, Sherlock Holmes–like, to guess the situation," (quoted in Shepherd, *Sherlock Holmes and the Case of Dr. Freud*, p. 9). Yet more important, as Calhoon suggests, Freud shares with the fictional detective the task of restoring meaning to a "pointillist universe" in which people, actions, and things have lost both connection and meaning ("The Detective and the Witch," p. 33). The film *The Seven Percent Solution*, directed by Herbert Ross in 1976, brings Freud and Holmes together; it is based on the novel by Nicholas Meyer.

16. See Moews, *Keaton: The Silent Features*, pp. 80–3, for a discussion of the film's references to Pickford, Valentino, and Barrymore. The Barrymore film is *Sherlock Holmes*, directed in 1922 by Alber Parker. Sherlock Jr.'s assistant, Gillette, is probably a reference to the U.S. actor and playwright William Gillette (1853–1937), who played Holmes for years on stage throughout his lifetime and in a film produced by Essanay in 1916.

17. Because of its interest in society's weak and vulnerable, melodrama has long interested feminist critics. Melodrama often places women and their suffering under patriarchy at its center, valorizing the "feminine" emotions of pity and vividly depicting male villainy. Moews provided the information about Veronal (*Keaton: The Silent Features*, p. 86).

18. For an analysis of these gags, along with a discussion of the film's use of melodrama, see Kevin W. Sweeney, "Parody and Comic

Revision in Keaton's Features" (paper delivered at the Society for Cinema Studies Conference, New York, March 1995).

19. The girl's mother appears briefly in the frame story but has no significant narrative function. Mary Pickford captured some of the contradictions inherent in this era of enormous change in women's status, which culminated in the ratification of the Nineteenth Amendment in 1920. On the one hand, she cultivated an innocent and girlish persona anchored in the past. (The nostalgia for this image of femininity was represented even more vividly by Shirley Temple in the 1930s.) Yet that persona belied Pickford's real power offscreen as a modern businesswoman and one of the four founders of United Artists.

20. Indeed, this voyeurism – true of all detectives – contributes even more to the whiff of depravity already surrounding Holmes, with his addiction to cocaine.

21. Truzzi, "Sherlock Holmes: Applied Social Psychologist," p. 71.

22. Calhoon, "The Detective and the Witch." See also Gian Paolo Caprettini, who writes: "The woman, who has the power of starting illogical (that is passionate) mechanisms in man's mind, must be strictly excluded from the sphere of analytical and abductive reasoning. . . . It is part of the Holmes-hero status that he can be defeated only by a woman, and only once" ("Peirce, Holmes, Popper," in *The Sign of Three,* ed. Eco and Sebeok, p. 149). (That woman is Irene Adler in *A Scandal in Bohemia.*) "Therefore the woman represents a kind of taboo, a prohibited, excluded space" (p. 151).

23. Moretti, *Signs Taken for Wonders,* p. 139.

24. René Girard, *Deceit, Desire and the Novel* (Baltimore: Johns Hopkins Press, 1965).

25. Eve Kosofsky Sedgwick, *Between Men: English Literature and Male Homosocial Desire* (New York: Columbia University Press, 1985), p. 1.

26. Douglas Fairbanks starred in a parody called *The Mystery of the Leaping Fish* (1916). There was even a *Sherlock Holmes, Junior* made in 1911, one of a number of child versions of the detective produced in the United States and Europe during the early teens. See Pohle, Jr., and Hart, *Sherlock Holmes on Screen,* esp. chap. 26, "The Apocryphal Adventures of Sherlock Holmes."

27. These quotes appear in Shepherd, *Sherlock Holmes and the Case of Dr. Freud,* p. 20.

28. Calhoon, "The Detective and the Witch," p. 33.

29. In "The Scandal in Bohemia," Doyle writes of Holmes as loathing

"every form of society with his whole Bohemian soul" (quoted in Caprettini, "Peirce, Holmes, Popper," p. 149).

30. See William Willeford, *The Fool and His Scepter: A Study of Clowns and Jesters and Their Audiences* (Evanston, IL: Northwestern University Press, 1969), esp. chap. 10, "The Fool and the Woman."

31. See Frank Krutnik, "A Spanner in the Works? Genre, Narrative and the Hollywood Comedian," in *Classical Hollywood Cinema*, ed. Karnick and Jenkins, pp. 17–38; and Steve Seidman, *Comedian Comedy: A Tradition in Hollywood Film* (Ann Arbor, MI: UMI Research, 1981).

32. Personal communication.

4 Passing Through the Equal Sign

FRACTAL MATHEMATICS IN *SHERLOCK JR.*

A great acrobat, like a great yogi, is always in balance. So is an equation, which must (by definition) represent an equality and balances perfectly on its equal sign. Keaton, acrobat extraordinaire, built his sight gags, his characters, and his films themselves on unique, quasi-mathematical structures that move back and forth between balance and imbalance – producing a playful cinematic tension that gives his films a unique, structuralist elegance and a matchless spiritual depth.

Imagine Keaton teetering on a ladder, pivoting dangerously on top of a tall fence, as he does in *Cops* (1922). Imagine the ladder oscillating back and forth, as Keaton pretends to lose his balance and regain it. Of course, he's not really losing his balance; this stunt requires perfect balance and precise acrobatic skill to achieve – and even greater talent to make funny.

I think of Keaton's ladder-balancing act as a kind of comic equation, a playful testing of the values on either side of a cinematic equal sign. (In fact, since the ladder is horizontal for most of the gag, it becomes the balance arm of a scale – a tool for equating objects on either side.) Keaton creates many of his most delightful stunts by manipulating the "numbers" arrayed at the ends of some such comic equation, pretending to unbal-

118

ance them in the same way he pretends to lose his balance at the top of the ladder. In the process, he reveals a profound spiritual balance at the center of his work.

Spiritual depth? Spiritual balance? Of course! The ladder stunt, like almost all the stunts in *Sherlock Jr.*, depends not on camera trickery or lab processing, but on Keaton's superb body work. At Keaton's master level, the line between yoga and acrobatics is hard to define; his physical balance clearly reflects an inner, spiritual balance. At the same time, Keaton is projecting a complex intellectual metaphysic (and an intricate structural conception of comic cause and effect) into physical reality, just as a swami might demonstrate an esoteric tantric meditation with the help of a yoga posture and a breathing pattern. It's exhilarating to see, as much for its cerebral rigor as its physical grace.

This is nowhere as true as it is in *Sherlock Jr.* The famous image of Keaton balancing on the handlebars of a riderless motorcycle, perfectly poised in a world of trouble, could be the central metaphor for his entire filmic career. This essay will look at the mathematical, dramatic, and spiritual equations that balance *Sherlock Jr.*

The opening epigram to *Sherlock Jr.* reads, "Don't try to do two things at once and expect to do justice to both." Here we find the first iteration of the film's primal, mathematical metaphor: two things, the two sides of an equation, Keaton as motion picture projectionist and amateur detective, equal and yet not-equal. Keaton will find an infinitude of ways to balance, unbalance, and rebalance this equation before the film is over.

Even the first line of dialogue underscores the duality: Keaton sits alone in the back of the theater, reading his detective textbook, and ignoring a pile of trash in the aisle. His boss snaps, "Say – Mr. Detective – before you clean up any mysteries – clean up this theater." Two kinds of cleaning, a connection, a conflict, an equivalency. Keaton starts cleaning up the trash, and as he sweeps the pile outside we see that the film he's showing is *Hearts and Pearls or the Lounge Lizard's Lost Love*. It's yet another equation, an equivalency connected by the Boolean[1] operator OR. Keaton strolls toward the candy store next to the theater. He wants to buy a box of candy for his girlfriend. Two boxes sit in the window, one costing one dollar and one costing three. It's a mathematical puzzle. Keaton has only two dollars, so he tries negotiating with the saleswoman. She is friendly but unyielding – and provides one of the moral poles of the film: numbers can't be manipulated. The price is the price. Three dollars equals three dollars, not two dollars, not one, not four. Ultimately, the equation has to balance.

Beaten by the math, Keaton returns to the trash pile – where he evolves a delicious variation on an ancient gag. A sticky piece of paper becomes attached to Keaton's broom, then his foot, then his hand. He removes it with the other hand, but it only sticks there. Chaplin could have rung changes on this chestnut for most of a two-reeler. Instead, Keaton invents a cerebral solution. He can't cheat the math, can't change the comedic numbers, so he invents a new kind of math: he lurks next to the doorway and when the owner emerges Keaton manages to place the sticky paper where he'll step on it – and walk away with it stuck to his shoe. Transformational math!

Now Keaton finds a dollar in the trash. Adding this to the two bucks he's already got, he can buy that three-dollar box of candy. But just as he's ready to go, a young woman arrives and reports that she lost a dollar. Keaton, still hoping to keep the dollar, asks her to describe it. This exchange is funny enough, but to make it even funnier the woman looks over Keaton's shoulder, cheating, as she describes the size and shape of the dollar bill, and even does a cute hand pantomime of the eagle. Keaton gives her the dollar. He has no choice: when she "identifies" the dollar, it balances an equation, making her hypothetical lost dollar identical with the real one that Keaton found. Her identification (even though it's arguably dishonest) is the equal sign.

But this set of equations is more complex than it seems. Now an older woman comes by, crying, and reports that she too lost a dollar. Having "proved" the equation the first time, Keaton has no choice but to abide by it. To save time, he performs the identification process we saw the young woman go through, duplicating it, creating a new equation (Keaton = young woman), gives the older woman one of his dollars, and borrows her hankie to wipe away a few tears of his own (crying woman = crying Keaton). Of course, this also means young woman = older woman.

The equations are still not perfectly balanced. A tough-looking guy appears and rummages through the trash. By now projectionist Keaton thinks he knows the game, so he reaches in his pocket and hands over his last buck without being asked. The math is too much for him. But director Keaton contradicts our expectations and unbalances the equation. The tough guy hands back the dollar contemptuously. Keaton's cash ain't nothin' but trash. Returning to the trash pile, the tough guy pulls out a wallet containing a fat wad of bills, fans the roll happily, and strides away counting his money. Keaton's simple equation has been subsumed in a larger, hairier ciphering. Perhaps this is an early presentiment of chaos theory.

Of course, there's a larger comedic equation at work here too, a general one, which I'll point out in passing.[2] It's a version of the basic Newtonian equation $PE = Mh = KE$ (potential energy = mass times elevation = kinetic energy [when converted]). The Keatonian equivalent defines the "capper," Keaton's primary modus operandi in comedy – which can also be considered a contract between Keaton and the audience. Keaton agrees to deliver a laugh, and sets it up. The audience laughs, feeling that the contract has been satisfied, and overlooks the fact that the equation is still way out of whack. We're not really done until $PE = KE$ = zero – which happens, in this case, when the tough guy finds the wad of cash, and you fall on your ass laughing because the true resolution (which you hadn't, until that moment, realized was required) has arrived.

In any case, Keaton is now down to a dollar. (Are you following the math? It's important.) All he can afford is the cheap box of candy, which he buys. But now, wanting his girl to think he's a big spender (and inspired, perhaps, by the chaotic tough guy), he takes a pen and changes the numeral 1 to the numeral 4. This heinous mathematical offense will prove his undoing. Changing numbers, falsifying data, is unforgivable. (Garbage in = garbage out.) Here Keaton the detective commits a serious crime, unbalancing a primal ethical equation. He will spend the rest of the film attempting to balance it again.

Keaton takes the candy and pays a visit to his girl. When he enters her house, he and the girl are caught in a striking two-shot, walking away from the camera, symmetrically balanced in the frame. The stair banister provides a vertical line between them, down the center of the frame: a romantic equal sign. This is probably what those *Cahiers du Cinema* critics like Jean-Luc Godard meant by mise-en-scène when they first mentioned this ineffable and virtually indefinable film term back in the 1960s. When Keaton's rival (identified only as "the sheik," common slang at the time for someone "fast" with the ladies) enters the house, his shot isn't nearly as elegant.

Sitting in the parlor with his girl, Keaton pointedly turns over the box of candy so she'll see the price tag. He's proud of his crime! But the sheik, watching from the hallway, observes Keaton's showboat move and determines to beat him at his own game. He's broke too, so he steals a watch from the pocket of a hanging jacket and rushes off to the pawnshop. This theft provides an intriguing, Hitchcockian reflection of Keaton's mathematical crime, and opens an equation connecting them. As in so many Hitchcock films, it equates the hero and the villain as wrongdoers. Hitchcock's habitual use of this dark equation refers back to the Catholic/Christian doctrine of original sin (according to which everyone is necessarily a wrongdoer); Keaton's use of it is lighter, merely suggesting that even the best of us mess up from time to time.

Keaton gives the girl a ring – but the stone is so small she has to squint to see it, so he loans her his detective's magnifying glass. This is a cheat too, of course, but it's an open one, which makes it more playful and less dangerous. It is a momentary, pretended loss of ethical balance, like Keaton's pretended loss of balance on top of the ladder, which raises the dramatic stakes and increases our enjoyment of the acrobatic stunt. Here, while his onscreen character tries to inflate the size and worth of his gift, the stratagem is so transparent that we half-expect the girl to laugh along with us.

Again in this shot we find Keaton and the girl perfectly balanced in the frame, facing the camera with parallel postures, making an elegant romantic equation. It shows they are well suited. Even their timid, stop-and-start attempts at hand holding are played in parallel, duplicated motions, the fun coming from the momentary variations in balance between their expressions and actions.

But now the sheik returns with a huge three-dollar box of candy. He takes the girl into the next room and draws the curtain. When Keaton joins them, he moves into a symmetrical three-shot in which the girl stands between the two men like an equal sign – at this moment an accurate image. But the sheik gets rid of Keaton by giving him a banana and shooing him out of the room.

Keaton eats the banana and places the peel on the ground, where he hopes to get the sheik to step on it. But his mean-spirited ploy is foiled; the sheik stops short. Worse yet, when Keaton becomes enraged at the sight of the sheik kissing the girl's hand and rushes in, he slips on the peel and falls. It's a terrific acrobatic flip in which Keaton falls back with both feet over his head and only one hand on the floor behind him, lands on his shoulders, kicks himself back into the air, and flips over onto his hands and knees before climbing to his feet! Needless to say, a feat like this would be unthinkable without perfect balance. The old banana skin equation (banana skin = comic fall) that Keaton tries to use on the sheik proves true as ever, only this time Keaton finds himself on the wrong end of the equal sign.

The theft of the watch is discovered. Keaton opens his detective book for help, but the sheik, reading over Keaton's shoulder, spots the line that advises "Search Everybody" and is inspired to plant the pawn ticket in Keaton's pocket. This action echoes the young woman's sneaking a look over Keaton's shoulder as she describes the lost dollar, and is just as "wrong," since it really represents burglarizing a value from one side of the equal sign (the information in the book) and slipping it surreptitiously onto the other side. This is neither ethically nor mathematically permissible; equivalency is not the same as theft.

When the girl's father (played by Joe Keaton) finds the four-dollar pawn ticket in Keaton's pocket, it is equal to the four-dollar price marked on Keaton's box of candy. This fatal equation damns him as a thief, and constitutes a perfectly appropriate payback for his crime of falsifying data. He really is guilty, although not of the felony for which he's convicted. As in Hitchcock, even a minor misstep can place you in grave jeopardy. The girl returns Keaton's ring, and he leaves in disgrace. This time they are both on the same side of the banister, the frame is unbalanced, the romantic equation deranged.

Keaton is determined to find the real thief with the help of his detective book. The next instruction is "Shadow Your Man Closely." The concept of a shadow, a duplicate image cast by an object, suggests its own ominous equation. And in the next series of shots, Keaton does indeed shadow the sheik closely, imitating his posture and movements with comic exactitude, as if an invisible equal sign connected them. Striding a scant foot or two behind, Keaton matches his quarry's stops, starts, hand motions, even a jaunty skip, and a neat bit with a cigarette: the sheik takes a puff and tosses it away; Keaton catches it, takes his own equivalent puff, and tosses it too. Here, again, the sequence gains impact through the "reality" of Keaton's performance; there's no cheating.

The shadow equation carries them across a street, through traffic, and into a train yard, where Keaton breaks the equation and ducks behind a freight car for cover – and is nearly hit when another freight car couples with a huge impact. The two cars end up perfectly balanced in the frame, with the coupling (another equal sign) at dead center. It's a dangerous stunt; Keaton makes it look so easy we forget that even a slight mistake in position or timing could have caused the car to squash him like a bug. He breaks out of the shadow equation only at risk.

Here, at the approximate midpoint of the film, Keaton places a very important equal sign. The inter-title reads: "As a detective he was all wet, so he went back to see what he could do to his other job." Keaton's character is about to move to the cinematic side of the equal sign. It will prove to be a profoundly consequential action.

Back at the pawnshop, the girl discovers that it was the sheik, not Keaton, who pawned the stolen watch. Now she knows that Keaton is innocent – but Keaton does not yet know that she knows. Up in the projection booth, he starts a showing of *Hearts and Pearls* – and promptly falls asleep.

In double exposure (the purest cinematic form of an equation, with both sides visible at the same time), Keaton's dream double emerges, looks at the film, and notices that it echoes his real-life dilemma. The double enters the theater, takes a seat for a while, and finally jumps into the "frame" to accost the villain.

Here begins one of Keaton's most brilliant (and most celebrated) sequences, an elegant series of mathematical variations in which Keaton's side of the equation (his position and posture) is static, while the other side of the equation (the filmic setting in which he finds himself) is constantly changing. Only the equivalency between them is fixed: the all-important cinematic equal sign.

Initially, the villain tosses Keaton out of the frame entirely. The shot cuts to a house front. Keaton climbs the stairs and knocks. No answer. He is on his way down the stairs when the shot cuts to a garden wall. Keaton falls. He tries to sit on a bench, but a cut puts him on a city street full of fast-moving cars. He falls again, and barely regains his feet when a cut places him on the edge of a precipitous cliff. Just as he gets his balance, a cut drops him into a jungle with lions. He runs, but a cut transports him to a desert, where a train nearly hits him. Exhausted, Keaton sits on a rise, but a cut turns it into a rock set in the pounding surf. Keaton dives into the water, but a cut causes him to land in a snowbank. He gets to his feet and attempts to lean against a tree, but a cut places him back at the garden wall, and he falls again. Finally, a fadeout dissolves into a scene in which the villain steals a strand of pearls.

This amazing sequence reveals a modern, existential vision in which change is constant but underlying principles hold. Balance can be maintained, *must* be maintained, but only through a flexible, inertia-less, Zen-level improvisation that welcomes the certainty of change as a joyful challenge, an invitation to a dance in which cause and effect are less important than motion and laughter.

It's an epiphanous moment for Keaton, a vision of eternal truths at the center of the universe. Now, having understood the quintessential nature of cinema – the certainty of change, twenty-four of them every second – Keaton can enter *Hearts and Pearls*. The falls and frightening dislocations punish him for his crime, balancing the equation (and the books) and returning him to a state of grace. For Keaton it's a journey *through* the equal sign. He is reborn as his double, Sherlock Jr., capable of reinventing himself as well as his problem, capable of solving the crime. He is enlightened, unlimited.

In the film-within-a-film, the bad guys are scheming to do away with the troublesome detective. Two nitro-loaded pool balls (number 13, of course) form their own hazardous equation. The villains will substitute one of the deadly balls for an innocuous one when Sherlock Jr. approaches the pool table. If that doesn't work, they have set up two symmetrical halberds, one of which is triggered to fall when Sherlock sits in a booby-trapped chair. All the deadly traps are pairs: more equations. And the very idea of a film-within-a-film refracting Keaton's real-life situation reiterates the idea of equivalency, forming a fractal mirror image and making another equation to be balanced.

Keaton, transfigured by his journey through the equal sign, is now formidable and impeccable. Note the extraordinary moment when he is about to sit on the booby-trapped chair. He stops a bare inch above the seat and floats, in matchless, motionless balance, for almost three full seconds before rising again. This accomplished body work echoes Keaton's underlying spiritual and intellectual mastery. This moment forms its own equation with the banana-peel fall and the matchless motorcycle-handlebars ride to come. There's a neat pas de trois involving Keaton, the bad guys, and two glasses of whiskey – one of which is poisoned. Keaton makes the most of the comic possibilities, working to balance and unbalance the equations involving two glasses and two villains.

One of the bad guys puts the deadly 13 ball in play, opening a potentially hazardous equation – but by now Keaton owns the equal sign. He observes the substitution in an overhead mirror, essentially looking over his own shoulder, providing a third iteration of the over-the-shoulder gag, but now appropriately transfigured. Then he executes an impossibly complicated series of pool shots in which he runs the table, hitting every ball except the nitro 13. Apparently, he has also become a master of Euclidean geometry and Newtonian motion physics. Keaton's math is unbeatable; he can get away with anything.

To make the point unmistakably clear, he follows this sequence with an extended example of comic filmmaking genius. To begin, Keaton escapes from a rooftop on which the villain has trapped him by riding a raised railroad gate to a gentle landing in the villain's car. Keaton, the master acrobat, is once again in perfect balance, sliding down gravity's rainbow, boss of the gravitic equal sign.

Before entering the bad guys' headquarters, Keaton prepares a slick getaway scheme by positioning a disguise in a window frame. Then, after strolling inside and snatching the stolen pearls, he dives through the window and is instantaneously transformed into an old lady. Here we see that Keaton has taken an almost godlike control of reality itself, moving in the blink of an eye from one side of the equal sign to the other, becoming his own disguised double. This is math with teeth!

The sequence is far from over. After the bad guys spot him, and he escapes by seeming to dive through his assistant's body and the wall of a house (more godlike magic here), two bad guys begin probing the wall. A revolving door appears, allowing Keaton to replace the two bad guys in the frame: a neat visual equation.

Still on the run, Keaton hitches a ride on the handlebars of a cop's motorcycle – but when the cop flies off after plunging through a ditch Keaton rides on alone, unaware and innocent. He careers through a series of obstacles – cross-traffic, curves, hay balers, lines of workmen who toss dirt in his face – always in perfect balance, moving in such profound equilibrium that he is in no danger. His self-possession here – physical, comical, spiritual, cinematic – is impeccable. This is his moment in history, and we all know it. It even seems that *he* knows it. Remember that Keaton actually did this stunt – or most of it anyway. (In the close-ups, Keaton's cycle appears to be attached to the camera car, which would make life much easier.) His acrobat's grace and intellectual rigor place him, for these timeless moments, not only at the center of every equation in Sherlock Jr., but at the center of film history. He has *become* the equal sign, the operator that draws everything around it into balance – even seventy years of time.

After he rescues the girl from the villain's clutches, Keaton makes his escape in a car with powerful "four wheel brakes." But when he uses them, the chassis of the car ends up in a lake, where it becomes (equals) a boat. Keaton, now the master of transformation, simply raises the convertible top as a sail to confirm his arrival on the far side of the car = boat equation.

Keaton emerges from the movie-within-a-movie and wakes up in the projection booth. The girl arrives and clears him. Keaton wants to kiss her, but he's too shy to proceed. So he simply imitates the clinch that's unreeling onscreen in his theater. It's the final equation of the film, and a very romantic one too, art imitating art. Only an onscreen dissolve to the "film" couple dandling their twin babies defeats him. Ironically, the only form of mathematics that he can't master is a very simple one: multiplication.

NOTES

1. Boolean algebra is a system of postulates and symbols (OR, AND, etc.) applicable to problems in logic.
2. I thank Dr. John Diebold for bringing it to my attention; this paragraph closely follows information I received from him (personal communication).

5 The Purple Rose of Keaton

Woody Allen's *The Purple Rose of Cairo,* released in 1984, met with great critical and commercial success. The film's turning point occurs when one of the characters in the film screened within the film becomes infatuated with a waitress in his movie house audience and steps out of the screen to court her. Startled by this action, the other reel characters begin to discuss their lives and the people in the audience in the manner that movie house audiences usually discuss characters in a film. Eventually the waitress accepts her upper-class suitor's invitation to step into the screen to experience his mode of life in reel space and time. The action is further punctuated by conversations between the reel characters and individuals in the movie house watching them.

Allen's collapse of the barriers between his film's reel world and his film's real world (which, of course, is just another reel world for Allen's viewers) cleverly addresses the question of how cinema creates as well as reflects values. The suspension of disbelief of many viewers to a great degree and of all viewers to some degree is such that characters in the reel world are responded to on the same or even stronger terms than people in the physical world of the viewer. Models of speech, dress, and behavior are adopted from reel worlds to become part of everyday life and are then often returned to the screen as reflections of existing cultural norms. Allen was justly hailed for dealing with complex issues in accessible and amusing terms. Almost no one noted that Buster Keaton had opened this discourse some sixty years earlier in *Sherlock Jr.*

Reducing *Sherlock Jr.* to merely a reflection on the film medium and that medium's relationship to working-class viewers would be a gross simplification to be sure. Considerably more goes on in the film technically, thematically, and theatrically. Keaton's film also offers historians of the cinema an example of the problems faced by filmmakers in transition from the two- and three-reelers of early silents to what became standard feature lengths. In this sense, although the five-reel *Sherlock Jr.* is too long for certain effects and too short for others, it offers its own particular configuration of time for Keaton-style comedy. Dealing with the social dimensions of the film's famed self-reflection on the nature of the medium does not negate these or other considerations, but to ignore or minimize them would be to belie the film's surprising complexity. Not everything is played strictly for laughs, and even when social commentary is not consciously intended, comic routines always remain imbued with social resonance.

The dramatic structure of *Sherlock Jr.* consists of three parts: a medium-length overture, a long main act, and a brief anticlimax. The overture, shot in a realistic style, portrays a working-class youth, employed as a movie house projectionist, who can never realize his personal vision in the world around him. The main act, a film-within-a-film, always imaginative, sometimes surrealistic, transforms the hapless youth into an invincible sleuth with incredible mental and physical powers. The anticlimax returns the hero to the projection booth, from which he directly copies into his immediate world the behavior he sees projected in the reel world he so recently was a part of. Boundaries are further shattered by his silent but direct discourse with the unseen audience of both of Keaton's fictive worlds.

The initial fifteen minutes or so of *Sherlock Jr.* are much like the cumbersome first chapters of many Victorian novels. A great deal of information essential to the development of the plot is transmitted, but the details unfold in a pedestrian and even ponderous manner. Few opportunities are available for the display of any of Keaton's strongest assets. Nearly any silent performer, comedian or not, could have played these scenes just as well. In decided contrast, the film-within-a-film is entirely dependent on Keaton's fabled athleticism, and the anticlimax on Keaton's trademark deadpan facial expressions.

THE REAL WORLD?

Our first view of the hero is that of a young man sitting in a movie theater with the house lights turned on. He is reading a manual on how to become a detective. The cue cards inform us that one cannot do two things at once and do them well, but the visual image is more specific: dreamy movie house projectionist reading escapist literature in the receiving hall of cinematic dreams. Clearly he is dissatisfied with who and where he is. He hopes to redefine himself, but his reveries are rudely interrupted when the owner of the theater orders him back to work. Although technically employed as a projectionist, he must also sweep the floors.

Going through the trash that the departed film audience has left behind, he begins to find crumpled dollar bills. A series of skits featuring returning patrons reveals the hero to be kind-hearted, overly polite, and not economically shrewd. Ultimately, he is left with a single dollar. In contrast, a disreputable character walks off with a wallet full of cash.

Dollar in hand, our hero sets off to purchase a gift for "the girl" (Kathryn McGuire), his sweetheart. Unable to buy the higher-priced items on display, he purchases a box of candy. Showing some ingenuity, he uses his pen to alter the one-dollar price tag so that it looks like four dollars. The girl, who cares little about the price of the candy, is delighted. As a portent of

FIGURE 12
Buster and his true love in *Go West* (1925). (Courtesy of KINO Video, New York.)

things to come, the two sit side by side and are so innocent they do not know how to proceed with their romance. Just touching hands is a task they cannot manage with any grace. Sherlock Jr. finally offers the girl a ring having a jewel so small that she needs his detective's magnifying glass to see it. Nonetheless, he has won the girl's heart.

A second visitor approaches the girl's home. He is the sheik (Ward Crane), a local rake whose desire for the girl is decidedly carnal. While spying on the sweethearts from the hallway, Crane discovers that the girl's father has left his vest on a rack. Crane steals a watch from the vest and hurries off to pawn it in order to raise cash. Returning to the girl's home with a large box of candy, he momentarily gains her attention. As Sherlock Jr. belatedly attempts to reassert himself, the father and his worker appear to announce that a watch has been stolen. Making every effort to show his cleverness, Sherlock Jr. reads in his how-to book that everyone must be searched. The crafty Crane foils this effort by slyly placing the pawn ticket in his rival's jacket pocket. The scene ends with the father banishing Keaton from his home.

Still enamored of the idea of being a sleuth, Sherlock Jr. waits outside his sweetheart's home for Crane to depart. Literally following every detailed instruction in his manual – another signal of things to come – the boy becomes an utter flop. In sequences that allow for some good physical humor, Keaton trails Crane to a railroad yard, where he is completely outwitted and nearly drowns in water released from a railroad water tower. Totally defeated, he returns to the movie house, where it is time for him to assume his duties. As his projector beams images into the hall below, he falls into a depressed sleep. A ghostlike apparition then separates from his sleeping body. This dream projectionist will become the hero of the reel world about to unwind.

THE REEL WORLD OF *HEARTS AND PEARLS*

Sherlock Jr.'s alter ego gazes out of the projection booth to observe a metamorphosis in *Hearts and Pearls,* the film being viewed below. The film's lovers are transfigured into the girl and the sheik, and the supporting characters into the father and his assistant. Failing to arouse the sleeping Sherlock Jr. from his slumber, the alter ego wanders into the theater to sit with the audience. Propelled by his mounting anger at seeing the girl and Crane touching, he runs on to the stage and leaps into the reel world. A startled Crane unceremoniously hurls the alter ego from the screen. Summoning all his resources, our hero lunges upward for a second assault.

The sequences that follow are narrative non sequiturs that could have been accidentally spliced in from another film. Consisting of a series of incidents unconnected to one another or anything else in the film, they place our hero in great physical danger in abruptly shifting scenarios that involve such elements as high ledges, ocean tides, hungry lions, snowdrifts, and steaming locomotives. The surreal nature of these segments is underscored by the circumstance that we are constantly informed that this is a film-within-a-film. The episodes are candidly shown as being projected on the screen being viewed by the film's movie house audience. Even the piano accompanist is clearly visible and the screen is framed by the columns and drapes associated with traditional proscenium staging. In some ways these scenes resemble the vaudeville skits once done in front of the curtain while the hidden stage was being rearranged for a major act. At best, they may be considered an exegesis of the hero's emotional chaos. He doesn't know where he is and survives by sheer instinct. A less charitable view is that these are comic vignettes that Keaton could not otherwise weave into the plot but did not have the artistic willpower to omit.

Without explanation the screen suddenly fills out, and we are back on the set of *Hearts and Pearls*. This reel home of Sherlock Jr.'s girlfriend, unlike the former one, is unabashedly upper class. Crane has stolen valuable pearls from the family, not a four-dollar watch, and the girl's father's employee, now a butler, is part of the criminal gang. When the distraught father decides to hire Sherlock Jr., "the world's greatest detective," Crane becomes panicky. With the assistance of his cohort, he devises three booby traps: a poisoned drink, a billiard ball that contains a bomb, and a chain rigged so that an ax falls to split an unwary sitter in two.

The Sherlock Jr. who enters this realm is no longer of the working class. The dreamer's sense of competence, of being "classy," indeed of having "class," requires a complete rejection of working-class dress, behavior, and taste. Consequently, he wears a top hat and a frock coat, and he matter-of-factly deposits his decorative cane with servants before sauntering about in a tuxedo adorned with a white vest, white breast-pocket handkerchief, and a sporty white bow tie. Without batting an eyelash, he instantly deduces that Crane is the thief. The traps set for him are not only artfully eluded but turned against their perpetrators. His invincibility appears categorical until Keaton chides the viewers by reminding us that the sleek sleuth has not yet located the missing pearls or the abducted girl.

Seen the next morning in his own home, which is more modest than that of the reel family of the girl, Sherlock Jr. is again dressed in a tux. Now he is aided by his own Dr. Watson, a mysterious Mr. Gillette, the same actor who plays the theater owner in the world outside this screen. Their power reversal, however, is far from complete. Gillette will appear periodically with magical devices required by Sherlock for one or another of his attempts to recover the pearls and free the girl. As the day wears on, Sherlock Jr.'s triumphs increasingly depend more on luck and magic than on cunning or skill. The closer Sherlock Jr. comes to success, in fact, the more he exhibits some of the ineptitude of the sleeping projectionist.

The climatic moments to a series of chase episodes occur when Sherlock Jr. has recovered the pearls and placed the rescued girl in a purloined convertible. Instead of getting her to a safe haven, he carelessly drives off the road into a lake. The couple is saved from drowning only when Sherlock Jr. keeps the car afloat by transforming the car's convertible top into a sail. Floating along romantically, Sherlock Jr. and the girl momentarily sit side by side in the manner they had in the parlor room of another reality. Their bliss turns to panic when the sail fails and the car/boat begins to sink. Sherlock Jr. of the tux has proved to be as wet a sleuth as Sherlock Jr. of the rail yard. Suddenly we are back in the projection booth as our awakening hero frantically flays his arms in the air like a man staving off drowning. A fitful glance out the projection booth window verifies that *Hearts and Pearls* is now back to its original cast. Sherlock Jr.'s reel world adventures have ended.

WHEN THE REAL MEETS THE REEL

The girl now enters the projection booth to inform Sherlock Jr. that she has solved the crime he was accused of and that her father has lifted the ban on his presence in their house.

She waits for the lover whom she has vindicated to respond. Sherlock Jr., however, is at a complete loss as to what constitutes an appropriate reaction. The series of cuts that follow contain some of the shrewdest and most economical cinematic commentary ever shot concerning the issue of how working-class film viewer's relate to the films they patronize.

A desperate Sherlock Jr. looks out of his booth and sees a similar love scene being played out on the screen. When the reel lover takes his sweetheart's hand into his own, Keaton takes the girl's hand in exactly the same way. Still at a loss as to how to proceed, he looks to the screen once more. The reel lover kisses his sweetheart's hand. Sherlock follows suit. Again, without reference to his own feelings, he looks to the screen for instruction. The reel lover now places a ring on his sweetheart's finger. Sherlock Jr. desperately fumbles in his vest, finds a ring, and places it on the girl's finger, again exactly in the manner he has seen on the screen. When the reel lover cups his sweetheart's face with his palms and kisses her lips, Keaton does likewise. The sequence ends with a dramatic flash forward on the screen showing the reel male as a father with two babies on his knees and his wife beside him. Keaton hesitates and looks quizzically to the audience. Perhaps his deadpan expression indicates he is not sure where or how these children were produced. Or perhaps he is finally questioning just how much of his destiny he wants dictated by the screen.

The viewers of both pairs of lovers are given considerable emotional distance and a chance for intellectual reflection by Keaton's choice of framing. The *Hearts and Pearls* lovers are frankly presented as characters in a film being viewed by a visible movie house audience seated in rows much like students at a college lecture. In contrast, Sherlock Jr. is spatially isolated. He is tightly bound by the square of the projection booth window, so that the audience does not see his entire body and sees even less of the girl, who stands slightly behind him. The images are further isolated in that the booth fills only three-quarters of the screen, the rest being blackened out.

With this staging, Keaton has established considerable distance between the two reel worlds and the real world watching. The immediate effect is to reassure the countless lovers in theaters everywhere that they are not wrong to accept emotional and sexual instruction from the screen. In ways he could not have foreseen, Keaton has wittily presaged an aspect of film culture that has grown ever stronger with the advent of sound, color, and giant screens. Film instructions obviously involve much more than examining the propriety of holding hands, the acceptable size of gifts, and when or how to kiss. Of greatest import is that these instructions, some complex, some simple, always reflect, directly and indirectly, the dominant culture as defined by its most prosperous classes.

THE PURPLE ROSE OF ALLEN

When Woody Allen took on some of these themes six decades later, his protagonist was not a male projectionist exploited by a theater owner, but a small town's most avid filmgoer, a waitress who is abused by her husband. Rather than the waitress immediately entering the reel world, a reel world innocent leaves the screen to experience her world. The reality crisis is given another dimension when the actor who plays the character from the reel world comes to coexist with his creation in the world of the waitress. The two facets of one identity become romantic rivals, but even as they vie with each other for her affections, both reflect the values of the privileged classes celebrated in their reel worlds.

The waitress is barren of independent imagination. Her working-class world is not to be explored for its own values and images. Certainly it is not to be celebrated. Instead, her world is fit only to be instructed by its betters, to be abandoned as soon as possible, and to be held captive by the images of mass media. Thus, *Sherlock Jr.* and *The Purple Rose of Cairo* may be considered cinematic bookends. The dreams of Keaton's projectionist and Allen's waitress interlock. Or if we remember that the projectionist and waitress are also beings of reel worlds, what is truly happening is that Allen's social observations echo or coincide with those of Keaton.

Allen concludes his tale with a second film-within-a-film. Before leaving town for what she hopes will be a better life somewhere else, his waitress, now estranged from her husband and unemployed, returns for one last visit to the local hall of dreams. Despite her recent adventures, the reel world has lost none of its power over her. She rapturously and uncritically watches Fred Astaire and Ginger Rogers dancing cheek to cheek. Fred wears a tux and carnation like those worn by Sherlock Jr. during his sojourn in the reel world, and Ginger is clad in a gown and wears jewels the female lead of *Hearts and Pearls* might own. They dance with a grace and style the projectionist and waitress can never hope to emulate in an elegant dinner club they will always be too poor to patronize.

6 Playing Detective

POSSIBLE SOLUTIONS TO THE PRODUCTION MYSTERIES OF *SHERLOCK JR.*

While sitting at home on Baker Street, I received a call from someone asking me to determine how Buster Keaton constructed one of his films, *Sherlock Jr.*, which was released back in April 1924.

Filling my pipe, I considered the difficulties of determining the film's construction. Today, one can study the production history of Buster Keaton's films only under considerable disadvantage. First, there are no written scripts for any of his independent films. Instead, Keaton and his production staff worked the ideas out verbally beforehand, with some possible improvising on the set during the filming. Second, there are no surviving production schedules for the films. Third, unlike Chaplin, who saved his outtakes for posterity, Keaton, like most directors, burned his. Fourth, neither Keaton nor his crew were ever asked about the production in any great detail, and all are now dead. Nevertheless, this was an easy case for me. Although there is no way to be absolutely sure, I believe there exists enough evidence on *Sherlock Jr.*, both written and present in the film itself, to suggest the order in which the movie was shot.

It seems that *Sherlock Jr.* was shot in roughly this sequence:

1. The latter half of *Hearts and Pearls*, including the crazy magical gags and the motorcycle ride. These scenes appear to have been directed by both Keaton and Roscoe "Fatty" Arbuckle.
2. The earlier half of *Hearts and Pearls* (the billiard game), which may or may not have been co-directed by Arbuckle. The remaining scenes were all directed solely by Keaton.
3. The famous projection sequence in which the boy falls asleep and his dream alter ego walks into the movie.
4. The latter part of the frame story (the stolen watch and the boy's chasing of the sheik).
5. Introductory material and the dollar-candy routine.

In other words, it appears that Buster shot *Sherlock Jr.* approximately in reverse order. Why do I think this?

First, because *Sherlock Jr.*, like *The Three Ages* (1923), naturally falls into three complete sections (the frame story, the projection sequence, and *Hearts and Pearls*), it is logical to assume that Buster shot the film as three complete short components. Second, because the latter part of *Sherlock Jr.* uses so many impossible gags, it seems likely that Keaton and staff would revert to their old formula for making two-reel comedies ("Make the beginning, then the ending, and the middle will take care of itself").[1] Third, since Keaton does not mention Arbuckle when discussing the making of the projection sequence, it must be assumed that the scene was shot after Arbuckle left.[2] Fourth, as Keaton apparently thought the frame story was of lesser importance, coupled with the fact that Buster broke his neck at the end of the train scene, it was probably shot last.

Confusing? Well, let us take it one step at a time.

EXHIBIT ONE: BUSTER BROKE HIS NECK DURING THE WATER TOWER SCENE

Perhaps the most telling piece of evidence is that Buster Keaton broke his neck during the making of *Sherlock Jr.* As his wife Eleanor recalled:

FIGURE 13
Roscoe Arbuckle's nephew, Al St. John (top left), appeared with
Keaton in *The High Sign* (1920). (Courtesy of KINO Video,
New York.)

The train went out from under him. He rode the water tower
down to the track. But he didn't realize how much force that
water had and it threw him against the railroad track with the
back of his head. He had a terrible headache. I think they
called off shooting for a few days anyway. Then he went back
to work, and that was the end of that until about twelve or
thirteen years later. He went in for a complete physical: X-rays
and the whole lot. And the doctor said, "When did you break
your neck?" He said, "I never broke my neck." He said, "Yes,
you did break your neck." Buster said, "Do you think it could

have been when I hit my head against the railroad track?" The doctor said, "Sounds reasonable to me."[3]

It is interesting that the point in the filmmaking where Buster broke his neck corresponds to the abrupt end of the boy's chasing of the sheik. The film goes immediately from the water tower scene into the projection dream sequence without any real transition. It may have been that Buster was forced by his injury to end the first chase early.[4] Further, even if Buster didn't know he'd broken his neck, he certainly knew he was injured. A Buster Keaton so badly injured that shooting had to be called off seems an unlikely candidate to jump off buildings, or ride on motorcycle handlebars, or perform any of the other crazy stunts Buster does in the latter part of the picture.

EXHIBIT TWO: CONFLICTING STATEMENTS CONCERNING ROSCOE ARBUCKLE'S DIRECTION OF *SHERLOCK JR.*

In *My Wonderful World of Slapstick,* Buster Keaton revealed that Roscoe Arbuckle directed some of *Sherlock Jr.* "The experiment," said Keaton, "was a failure. Roscoe was irritable, impatient, and snapped at everyone in the company. He had my leading lady, Kathryn McGuire, in tears a dozen times each day." Keaton goes on to say that, in order to pull Arbuckle off *Sherlock Jr.,* he talked Marion Davies into having Hearst offer Arbuckle the directing role for *The Red Mill,* a more prestigious film costing over a million dollars to make. Torn between directing *Sherlock Jr.* and *The Red Mill,* Roscoe bowed out after being told, "Grab this big chance, Roscoe. Buster will finish it himself."[5]

Keaton changed this story slightly a couple of years later when he was interviewed by Kevin Brownlow for *The Parade's Gone By . . .* (1968), saying that Arbuckle worked on *Sherlock Jr.* for only three days, and the material Arbuckle filmed was later scrapped. From there, Keaton repeats to Brownlow *The Red Mill* story.[6] "Perhaps Keaton's memory was simply failing him," David Yallop wrote in *The Day the Laughter Stopped.* "Nearly three years elapsed between the filming of *Sherlock Jr.*, and the filming of *The Red Mill* (1927), and according to Doris Deane, who was on the set while *Sherlock* was made, Roscoe directed the picture from start to finish, and provided the story idea as well."[7]

Still another version of the story was that of Keaton's widow, Eleanor, in Andy Edmond's *Frame Up*. Eleanor says that Arbuckle "was so bitter, and so hurt, and so torn up that nothing was funny. Buster just had to take him off the film. He was so broken he wasn't getting things done right, he couldn't tell what was funny, and what wasn't funny. He snapped at everyone. Buster just wasn't able to use him. It was sad. But they remained close friends until the end. Buster used him on other pictures, but he didn't get credit."[8]

So these conflicting statements leave us with three distinct possibilities:

(1) Arbuckle was removed from *Sherlock Jr.* after only three days of shooting,
(2) Arbuckle directed *Sherlock Jr.* from start to finish, or
(3) Arbuckle was removed somewhere between (1) and (2).

Considering Arbuckle's circumstances and Keaton's close relationship to him, it seems highly unlikely that Buster would have removed Roscoe after only three days. Therefore, it is fairly easy to discount hypothesis (1).

A slightly better case, however, can be made for hypothesis (2). Arbuckle and Keaton had already made a "dream" film called *Goodnight Night, Nurse!* (1918). And Roscoe had played with surrealistic "dream" ideas as early as *He Did and He Didn't* (1916). Further, according to Yallop, Arbuckle contributed ideas to *The Frozen North* (1922), Keaton's lampoon of movie cowboy William S. Hart.[9] That short ends with Buster being awakened in a theater by an attendant, who says, "Wake up, the movie's over." Buster looks up to a title that says, "Yes, The End."[10] So there is a fair chance that it was Roscoe who came up with the idea for *Sherlock*

FIGURE 14
Keaton's lampoon of movie cowboy William S. Hart, *The Frozen North* (1922), included ideas contributed by Roscoe Arbuckle. (Courtesy of KINO Video, New York.)

Jr. However, if Arbuckle had fully co-directed the film, it seems extremely likely that Buster Keaton – Arbuckle's best friend – would have placed Roscoe Arbuckle's name on the credits. It should be noted that Arbuckle and Keaton remained the best of friends until Roscoe's death in 1933. In fact, in 1925, only a year after *Sherlock Jr.* was made, Buster was the best man at Arbuckle's wedding to his second wife, Doris Deane.

Both Keaton and Arbuckle obviously wanted Roscoe to succeed in directing *Sherlock Jr.*, meaning that a reasonable period would have gone by before they would have given up on the idea. For the same reason – Keaton wanting Arbuckle to succeed in forging a comeback after the scandal (see note 2) – it is equally clear that had Arbuckle broken down near the end of the shooting of *Sherlock Jr.*, Buster would have stuck it out with him to the end. Therefore, the only acceptable conclusion is hypothesis (3), that Keaton pulled Arbuckle sometime between (1) and (2), most likely during the first two to three weeks of shooting, probably by mutual consent.

EXHIBIT THREE: ARBUCKLE DIRECTING KATHRYN MCGUIRE

In his autobiography, Buster Keaton stresses that his leading lady, Kathryn McGuire, in particular had problems working with Arbuckle. In an interview with Christopher Bishop, Keaton says that co-directors directed the scenes in which he did not appear.[11] If one eliminates all scenes except those in which McGuire appears and Keaton does not, one is left with only two scenes of significance. The first is the one at Goldman's Pawn Shop at the end of the frame story, in which McGuire solves the crime of her father's stolen watch. It is a standard, noncomic scene that probably would not have caused much stress for Arbuckle. The second scene is the one in which she is abducted by her butler (played by Erwin Connelly).[12] The butler carries her off to a deserted shack and implies that he is going to rape her. If Roscoe Arbuckle, a man banned from Hollywood because he was falsely accused of rape/murder, had to direct this scene, it is easy to see how it could have caused him to crack. And I believe that is what happened.

EXHIBIT FOUR: THE MOTORCYCLE RIDE

In *Comedy Films, 1894–1954,* John Montgomery states, "While making *Sherlock Jr.*, Keaton had to ride a motorcycle while sitting on the handlebars. He hit both cameras, knocked down the director, and collided with a car."[13] Keaton knocked down the director. Since Keaton could not have run over himself, it seems safe to assume he knocked down Roscoe Arbuckle. As the motorcycle ride happens in the final reel (as does McGuire's abduction scene), I believe it is established that Arbuckle directed at least part of the *Hearts and Pearls* portion of the film.

If one accepts that Arbuckle directed both McGuire's abduction scene and the motorcycle ride (both late in the film), and if one accepts that Arbuckle directed at least the scenes shot early in the picture, there can be only one conclusion: *Sherlock Jr.* was shot out of sequence.

EXHIBITS FIVE: KEATON'S PRODUCTION METHODS ON HIS SHORT FILMS

That *Sherlock Jr.* was made out of sequence is not a startling observation. According to Keaton, most or all of his short films – made between 1920 and 1923 – were created in this way:

Somebody would come up with an idea. "Here's a good start," we'd say. We skipped the middle. We never paid any attention to the middle. We immediately went to the finish. We worked on the finish and if we get a finish that we're all satisfied with, then we'll go back and work on the middle. For some reason, the middle always took care of itself.[14]

EXHIBITS SIX AND SEVEN: *THE THREE AGES* AND *OUR HOSPITALITY*

Harold Lloyd's huge success with his first full-length film, *Grandma's Boy* (1922), appears to have been the major influence on Keaton's making the jump into features. Although Keaton had pressed his producer, Joe Schenck, to make features much earlier, it was not until after Lloyd had established feature comedy as a commercial success with *Grandma's Boy*, *Doctor Jack* (1922), and *Safety Last* (1923) that Keaton was given the go ahead to do so.

During this period, Harold Lloyd was also shooting films out of sequence. In *Safety Last,* for example, Lloyd first filmed the famous skyscraper climb, then went back with his writers to work out the reason Harold did it.

Keaton eased his transition from shorts to features by paro-

FIGURE 15
With *Our Hospitality* (1923), Keaton dropped wildly "impossible" gags from his films. (Courtesy of KINO Video, New York.)

dying D. W. Griffith's *Intolerance* with his own version of love through history, *The Three Ages*. Instead of making one six-reel comedy, Keaton made three short films, cleverly woven together. However, contrary to common belief, *The Three Ages* does not break down evenly into three two-reelers (which, according to legend, would have been released separately had the film failed, much as Griffith's *Intolerance* had been released when it bombed at the box office). Using a stopwatch, I found that the modern story in *The Three Ages* takes about twenty-seven minutes of the one-hour film, while the Roman story lasts about twenty, and the Stone Age lasts only about thirteen minutes.

As noted, Keaton filmed *The Three Ages* in three blocks: apparently the modern story came first, as it is the longest and has the most difficult gags; then the Roman age, with Keaton creating parallel gags between the two in order to link both in the audience's mind; and finally the shorter caveman story, again with linking gags.

Dissatisfied with the "cartoonish" quality of *The Three Ages,* for *Our Hospitality* Keaton replaced Eddie Cline (his co-director through most of the shorts) with feature comedy director Jack Blystone, who was brought in to help give the film a more balanced tone (meaning less slapstick). Perhaps influenced by Lloyd's *Grandma's Boy* (with both Keaton and Lloyd being influenced by the 1921 dramatic hit *Tol'able David*), *Our Hospitality* is set in 1830, somewhere near the Virginia–Kentucky border. With *Hospitality,* Keaton dropped wildly "impossible" gags from his films:

> After we stopped making wild two-reelers and got into feature-length pictures, our scenario boys had to be story-conscious. We couldn't tell any far-fetched stories. We couldn't do farce comedy, for instance. It would have been poison to us. An audience wanted to believe every story we told them. Well, that eliminated farce comedy and burlesque. The only time we could do something out of the ordinary had to be in a dream sequence, or in a vision.[15]

EXHIBIT EIGHT: KEATON'S THINKING BEHIND THE MAKING OF *SHERLOCK JR.*

Keaton discussed his reasoning for making *Sherlock Jr.* with Kevin Brownlow:

> Now I laid out a few of these tricks. Some of these tricks I knew from the stage. I got that batch of stuff together, and said, "I can't do it and tell a legitimate story." Because they're illusions, some are clown gags, some Houdini, some Ching-Ling-Fu [Shung Li Fou]. It's got to come in a dream. To get what we're after [you've] got to be a projectionist in a projecting room. Once you fall asleep, you visualize yourself as one of the important characters in the picture you're showing. And [you]

go down, out of that projecting room, go down there, walk up onto the screen and become a part of it. Now you tell your whole story.[16]

This appears to mildly contradict Buster's statements to John Gillett. When asked about the projection sequence, Buster said:

That was the reason for making the whole picture. Just that one situation, that a motion picture projectionist in a theatre goes to sleep and visualizes himself getting mixed up with the characters on the screen into my (the projectionist's) characters then I've got my plot. Now to make it work was another thing; and after that picture was made every cameraman in Hollywood spent more than one night watching it and trying to figure out those scenes.[17]

This leaves a final question: did Keaton shoot the projection sequence or *Hearts and Pearls?*

EXHIBITS NINE AND TEN: COSTUMES AND MATCHING SCENES

The beauty of the projection sequence lies in the ability of Keaton and his cameraman, Elgin Lessley, to match and cut the scene perfectly. Ironically, a similar matching scene in the film's final sequence gives away the solution to the problem. At the end of the dream, Sherlock Jr. is saving the girl by holding on to her while swimming. At this point, the boy wakes up after falling off his stool while holding on to the projector. To have this scene, Keaton must have shot the scene in the water first. Otherwise, he couldn't have matched the scenes!

Further, earlier when the dream figure first splits from the sleeping boy, he reacts to shots of the girl, the sheik, and the girl's father, already in *Hearts and Pearls* costume, becoming characters in the dream film. Logically, Keaton would have shot all these scenes in the projection room at the same time. Just as logically, Keaton's reaction shots in the projection room would have been made after *Hearts and Pearls* had been completed.

FIGURE 16
With *The Navigator* (1924) Keaton completed his transition from
the comedy short to the comedy feature. (Courtesy of KINO
Video, New York.)

Therefore, the projection sequences must have been shot after
Hearts and Pearls, but, as shown above, before the frame story.

CONCLUSION

Keaton created *Sherlock Jr.* in more or less reverse order. Because of Buster's neck injury, his problems with Arbuckle,

his statements concerning the construction of his shorts, and *Sherlock Jr.*'s multilayered format, this seems the only logical conclusion.

It is elementary. Keaton's retrograde shooting of *Sherlock Jr.* is a logical progression of a young filmmaker making the final transitions from the comedy short into the comedy feature. Although the seams in *The Three Ages* have an *Intolerance*-like visibility, the seams in *Sherlock Jr.* are less noticeable and would be practically invisible in Keaton's following features, starting with *The Navigator* (1924) and culminating with his masterpiece, *The General* (1926/7).[18]

In many ways, *Sherlock Jr.* was Keaton's fond farewell to the comedy short. This was the last film in which Keaton would be able to use outrageous "cartoon" gags. More important, it was the last time we could see Keaton's "Buster" as purely "Buster," the character we had enjoyed in the shorts. From this point, there would still be Keaton films, but they would never seem quite the same. Like the boy turning into Sherlock Jr., Buster Keaton had metamorphosed as well.[19]

NOTES

1. Buster Keaton to Kevin Brownlow in Brownlow's *The Parade's Gone By . . .* (New York: Knopf, 1968), p. 481.
2. The reader should know something about Roscoe Arbuckle and his close connections to Keaton to fully appreciate their relationship. Brought to Keystone in 1913 to replace the departing Fred Mace, Arbuckle soon became a mainstay of the Mack Sennett organization. But like Chaplin, he strained for creative freedom. In 1916, Sennett gave Arbuckle an independent unit in New Jersey, but at the end of that year, Arbuckle broke with Sennett for good. It was while Arbuckle was making his first completely independent film, *The Butcher Boy* (1917), that Buster Keaton wandered into movie making. Keaton was talked into visiting the Arbuckle set after bumping into Arbuckle's publicity man, Lou Anger, at Eighth and Broadway. While on the set, he shot a scene and liked it so much he tore up a $250 a week theatrical contract to work for Arbuckle at one-sixth the pay.

At the Arbuckle company – Comique – Keaton quickly went from being a featured player in *The Butcher Boy* and *Fatty at Coney Island* (1917), to second banana, gag writer, and assistant director for *Out West* and *Moonshine* (both 1918), to full co-star in *Back Stage* and *The Garage* (both 1919). Keaton's rise was even faster than it appears, as he served in the army in Europe for ten months during World War I.

After completing *The Garage*, Arbuckle was awarded a multi-million-dollar acting contract for features – the largest for any actor up to that time. With Arbuckle's departure from Comique, Keaton inherited control of the company, with which, after establishing himself as a star in the feature *The Saphead* (1920), he started cranking out masterpieces, beginning with *One Week* (1920).

Keaton and Arbuckle remained close friends. Keaton did a bit as an Indian in Arbuckle's first feature, *The Round-Up* (1920). Likewise, Arbuckle's nephew, Al St. John, appeared in Keaton's *The High Sign* (filmed 1920, released 1921), and Roscoe's multitalented dog, Luke, had a featured role in Keaton's fourth short, *The Scarecrow* (1920). Throughout this period, Keaton constantly asked and received advice from his mentor. "But one day in September 1921," Buster Keaton wrote in *My Wonderful World of Slapstick* (New York: Doubleday, 1960), "all of the laughter stopped. Overnight, what had been innocent fun was suddenly being denounced as 'another Hollywood drunken orgy' or 'one more shocking example of sex depravity.' The day our laughter stopped was the day Roscoe Arbuckle was accused of having caused the death of Virginia Rappé, a Hollywood bit player and girl about town, in his suite at the St. Francis Hotel, in San Francisco."

The accusations against Arbuckle turned out to be false. (The prosecution, led by a district attorney running for higher office who was determined to bring Arbuckle to trial, dropped the charges from rape/murder to manslaughter.) On cross-examination, the prosecution's case disintegrated into a tissue of lies. Nevertheless, there were three trials. Arbuckle's arrest caused the press, led by yellow journalist William Randolph Hearst, to sensationalize the case to such a degree (even to a greater extent than the recent O. J. Simpson affair) that a fair trial was impossible. One juror refused to listen to testimony, holding her hands over her ears, and said she would cast a guilty vote "until Hell froze over." After two hung juries, the third jury acquitted Arbuckle in six minutes, during five of which the jury spent composing a statement declaring that Arbuckle deserved an apology (see David A. Yallop, *The Day the*

Laughter Stopped: The True Story of Fatty Arbuckle [New York: St. Martin's Press, 1976], pp. 105–255).

Despite his innocence, Arbuckle was blacklisted from the screen for the next eleven years, allowed to work as a director only under an alias. Perhaps symbolically, he chose his father's name, "William Goodrich."

Not everyone abandoned Arbuckle. Keaton gave him 25 percent of the net profits of his films. Furthermore, a corporation called Reel Comedies Incorporated was financed by Keaton's and five other production firms for the sole purpose of allowing Arbuckle to direct two-reelers distributed by Educational Pictures through the 1920s. (Keaton even made a cameo appearance in the Arbuckle-directed *The Iron Mule* [1925].) Keaton's attempt to help Arbuckle by having him direct *Sherlock Jr.*, however, may have backfired so badly that it further damaged Arbuckle's reputation. After Keaton talked Marion Davies into having Arbuckle direct (as "William Goodrich") *The Red Mill* in 1927, King Vidor was called in to "assist" Roscoe because of "unspecified problems" (see Andy Edmonds, *Frame Up: The Untold Story of Roscoe "Fatty" Arbuckle* [New York: Morrow, 1991], p. 266).

3. Eleanor Keaton in *Buster Keaton: A Hard Act to Follow*, three video tapes (London: Thames Television PLC, 1987).

4. It is intriguing to speculate about what *Sherlock Jr.* would have been like had the accident not occurred. Logically, the film should have consisted of six reels instead of five. It appears that the original plan involved a longer chase sequence between the boy and the sheik, perhaps with the boy riding a bicycle. This would have kept up the parallel dream "trade-ups" between the boy and Sherlock, as described in Daniel Moews, *Keaton: The Silent Features Close Up* (Berkeley: University of California Press, 1977), pp. 75–99.

There are other reasons to think a sixth reel was planned. In *From Hand to Mouth* (1919), a film that appears to have had a strong influence on both Keaton's *Sherlock Jr.* and *Cops* (1922), Harold Lloyd chases a group of kidnappers on a bicycle, at one point riding on the handlebars. Furthermore, Arbuckle's nephew, Al St. John, was a trick-bicycle specialist, which Arbuckle may have capitalized on in the early stages of the process. (Arbuckle and/or St. John may have also supplied the original height-comedy gags for *The Three Ages*, since St. John used the same locations in *Special Delivery* [1922].)

5. Buster Keaton, *My Wonderful World of Slapstick* (New York: Doubleday, 1960).

6. Kevin Brownlow, *The Parade's Gone By . . .* (New York: Knopf, 1968).
7. Yallop, *The Day the Laughter Stopped,* p. 278.
8. Edmonds, *Frame Up,* p. 261.
9. Yallop, *The Day the Laughter Stopped.*
10. The other Keaton short films that involve dreams are *Convict 13* (1920), *The Haunted House* (1921), *The Play House* (1922), *Day Dreams* (1922), and *The Love Nest* (1923).
11. Christopher Bishop, "An Interview with Buster Keaton," *Film Quarterly* 12:1 (Fall 1958): 15–22.
12. Keaton and his writers (Jean Havez, Joe Mitchell, and Clyde Bruckman) apparently had trouble translating Connelly's butler role into the frame story. The role is laughed off with the title: "The girl's father had nothing to do so he got a hired man to help him."
13. John Montgomery, *Comedy Films, 1894–1954* (London: George Allen & Unwin, 1954), p. 141.
14. Keaton to Brownlow, *The Parade's Gone By . . . ,* p. 481.
15. Ibid.
16. Buster Keaton in *A Hard Act to Follow.*
17. John Gillett and James Blue, "Keaton at Venice," *Sight and Sound* 35:1 (Winter 1965): 26–30.
18. Almost invisible, but not quite. In *Keaton: The Silent Features Close Up,* Daniel Moews discusses the symmetrical patterns (first-half failures vs. second-half successes) throughout Keaton's features.
19. The following are excerpts from Bishop's "An Interview with Buster Keaton," in which Keaton gave his most detailed comments on the subject of *Sherlock Jr:*

    Of the features, which is your favorite?

    I have two – *The Navigator* and *The General.*

    How do you rate "Sherlock Jr." now?

    I like *Sherlock.* It was a good picture for me. It was the trickiest of all pictures I ever made because there were so many camera tricks and illusions. We spent an awful lot of time getting those scenes.

    How did you ever do the scene on the motorcycle? Is that a camera trick, or were you actually –

    No, there's no camera trick there.

    There is one shot where you can see the motorcycle from a distance and see that it isn't attached to anything. How did you manage to learn to do that?

    I'd just go out and learn to handle a motorcycle on the handlebars. It wasn't easy to keep a balance. I got some nice spills, though, from that thing.

    How did the scripts for these features evolve?

Well, now we will go back to our type of pictures. Now when I say "our type" you've got three people who were making them at that time: Chaplin, Harold Lloyd, and myself. Until I left my own studio and went to MGM – where it was a different proposition – we never had a script.

You never had any kind of a shooting script?

We never had a script. We didn't work by one. We just got to talking about a story and laying out all the material that we could think of, and then got it all put together – everybody connected with our company knew what we were going to shoot, anyway, and we didn't have a schedule.

How long did it take you to shoot a feature in the mid-20s?

We averaged about eight weeks of shooting.

About the dream sequence in "Sherlock Jr.," was this something that you thought of on the spur of the moment, or something that had been planned out ahead?

No, it was planned out ahead because we had to build a set for that one.

How was that done – did you have an actual screen beforehand on which the characters were appearing?

No. We built what looked like a motion picture screen and actually built a stage into that frame but lit it in such a way that it looked like a motion picture being projected on a screen. But it was real actors and light effect gave us the illusion, so I could go out of semi-darkness into that well-lit screen right from the front row of the theater right into the picture.

Then when it came to the scene changing on me when I got up there, that was a case of timing and on every one of those things we would measure the distance to the fraction of an inch from the camera to where I was standing, also with a surveying outfit to get the exact height and angle so that there wouldn't be a fraction of an inch missing on me, and then changed the setting to what we wanted it to be and I got back into that same spot and it overlapped the action to get the effect of the scene changing.

Which was the most popular of your features?

My biggest money maker was *The Navigator*. And next to that was *The General*.

How did "Sherlock Jr." stand up?

Hospitality outgrossed it, *Battling Butler* outgrossed it, *College* outgrossed it, *Steamboat Bill* outgrossed it. And then at MGM both *The Cameraman* and *Spite Marriage* outgrossed it. It was all right, it was a money maker, but it wasn't one of the big ones. Maybe it was because at the time it was released the audience didn't pay so much attention to the trick stunts that were in the picture.

How about the total gross on an average silent feature of yours?

We'd average between a million and a half and two million.

According to Tom Dardis (*Keaton: The Man Who Wouldn't Lie Down* [New York: Limelight Editions, 1988] and *Harold Lloyd: The Man on the Clock* [New York: Viking Press, 1983]), *Sherlock Jr.*

grossed $448,337; *The Navigator*, $680,406; *The General*, $474,264; *Our Hospitality*, $537,844; *Battling Butler*, $749,201; *College*, $423,808; *Steamboat Bill Jr.*, $358,839; *The Cameraman*, $797,000; and *Spite Marriage*, $701,000. Overall, of the twelve silent features Keaton starred in between 1923 and 1929, *Sherlock Jr.* ranks tenth in total grosses, ahead of both *College* and *Steamboat Bill Jr.*, and only $26,000 less than *The General*.

Most disturbing about Keaton's statements concerning his overall grosses is not so much that he exaggerated them as that he appears to have re-ranked them in an order more to his liking, placing two personal favorites – *The Navigator* and *The General* – at the top. He dropped *Sherlock Jr.*, on the other hand, to the bottom of the list. This suggests that perhaps Keaton didn't care much for the movie, most likely because of the problems Keaton faced during its filming.

Filmography

1917

The Butcher Boy
Story: Joe Roach
Scenario: Roscoe Arbuckle
Scenario editing: Herbert Warren
Director: Roscoe Arbuckle
Photography: Frank D. Williams
Producer: Joseph M. Schenck
Production company/distributor: Comique/Paramount
Cast: Roscoe "Fatty" Arbuckle, Buster Keaton, Al St. John, Arthur
   Earle, Josephine Stevens, Agnes Neilson, Joe Bordeau, Luke
   (the dog)

The Rough House
Story: Joe Roach
Scenario: Roscoe Arbuckle
Scenario editing: Herbert Warren
Director: Roscoe Arbuckle
Photography: Frank D. Williams
Producer: Joseph M. Schenck
Production company/distributor: Comique/Paramount

Cast: Roscoe "Fatty" Arbuckle, Buster Keaton, Al St. John, Alice Lake, Glen Cavender

His Wedding Night
Story: Joe Roach
Scenario: Roscoe Arbuckle
Scenario editing: Herbert Warren
Director: Roscoe Arbuckle
Photography: George Peters
Producer: Joseph M. Schenck
Production company/distributor: Comique/Paramount
Cast: Roscoe "Fatty" Arbuckle, Buster Keaton, Al St. John, Alice Mann, Arthur Earle

Oh Doctor!
Scenario: Jean Havez
Scenario editing: Herbert Warren
Director: Roscoe Arbuckle
Photography: George Peters
Producer: Joseph M. Schenck
Production company/distributor: Comique/Paramount
Cast: Roscoe "Fatty" Arbuckle, Buster Keaton, Al St. John, Alice Mann

Fatty at Coney Island
Scenario: Roscoe Arbuckle
Scenario editing: Herbert Warren
Director: Roscoe Arbuckle
Photography: George Peters
Producer: Joseph M. Schenck
Production company/distributor: Comique/Paramount
Cast: Roscoe "Fatty" Arbuckle, Buster Keaton, Al St. John, Alice Mann, Agnes Neilson, Joe Bordeau, James Bryant

A Country Hero
Scenario: Roscoe Arbuckle
Scenario editing: Herbert Warren
Director: Roscoe Arbuckle
Photography: George Peters
Producer: Joseph M. Schenck
Production company/distributor: Comique/Paramount
Cast: Roscoe "Fatty" Arbuckle, Buster Keaton, Joe Keaton, Alice Lake, Al St. John

1918

Out West
Scenario: Natalie Talmadge (?)
Scenario editing: Herbert Warren
Director: Roscoe Arbuckle
Photography: George Peters
Producer: Joseph M. Schenck
Production company/distributor: Comique/Paramount
Cast: Roscoe "Fatty" Arbuckle, Buster Keaton, Al St. John, Alice Lake

The Bell Boy
Scenario: Roscoe Arbuckle
Scenario editing: Herbert Warren
Director: Roscoe Arbuckle
Photography: George Peters
Producer: Joseph M. Schenck
Production company/distributor: Comique/Paramount
Cast: Roscoe "Fatty" Arbuckle, Buster Keaton, Al St. John, Alice Lake,
    Joe Keaton, Charles Dudley

Moonshine
Scenario: Roscoe Arbuckle
Scenario editing: Herbert Warren
Director: Roscoe Arbuckle
Photography: George Peters
Producer: Joseph M. Schenck
Production company/distributor: Comique/Paramount
Cast: Roscoe "Fatty" Arbuckle, Buster Keaton, Al St. John, Alice Lake,
    Charles Dudley, Joe Bordeau

Good Night, Nurse!
Scenario: Roscoe Arbuckle
Scenario editing: Herbert Warren
Director: Roscoe Arbuckle
Photography: George Peters
Producer: Joseph M. Schenck
Production company/distributor: Comique/Paramount
Cast: Roscoe "Fatty" Arbuckle, Buster Keaton, Al St. John, Alice Lake,
    Kate Price, Joe Keaton, Joe Bordeau

The Cook
Scenario: Roscoe Arbuckle
Scenario editing: Herbert Warren
Director: Roscoe Arbuckle

Photography: George Peters
Producer: Joseph M. Schenck
Production company/distributor: Comique/Paramount
Cast: Roscoe "Fatty" Arbuckle, Buster Keaton, Alice Lake, Al St. John, Glen Cavender, Luke (the dog)

1919

Back Stage
Scenario: Jean Havez
Director: Roscoe Arbuckle
Photography: Elgin Lessley
Producer: Joseph M. Schenck
Production company/distributor: Comique/Paramount
Cast: Roscoe "Fatty" Arbuckle, Buster Keaton and Al St. John, Molly Malone, John Coogan

The Hayseed
Scenario: Jean Havez
Director: Roscoe Arbuckle
Photography: Elgin Lessley
Producer: Joseph M. Schenck
Production company/distributor: Comique/Paramount
Cast: Roscoe "Fatty" Arbuckle, Buster Keaton, John Coogan, Molly Malone, Luke (the dog)

1920

The Garage
Scenario: Jean Havez
Director: Roscoe Arbuckle
Photography: Elgin Lessley
Producer: Joseph M. Schenck
Production company/distributor: Comique/Paramount
Cast: Roscoe "Fatty" Arbuckle, Buster Keaton, Molly Malone, Harry McCoy, Daniel Crimmins, Luke (the dog), Molly Moran, Monty Banks

KEATON'S SILENT SHORTS (1920–1923)
1920

One Week
Script: Buster Keaton, Eddie Cline
Director: Buster Keaton, Eddie Cline

Technical director: Fred Gabourie
Photography: Elgin Lessley
Producer: Joseph M. Schenck
Production company/distributor: Comique/Metro
Cast: Buster Keaton, Sybil Seeley, Joe Roberts

Convict 13
Script: Buster Keaton, Eddie Cline
Director: Buster Keaton, Eddie Cline
Technical director: Fred Gabourie
Photography: Elgin Lessley
Producer: Joseph M. Schenck
Production company/distributor: Comique/Metro
Cast: Buster Keaton, Sybil Seeley, Joe Roberts, Eddie Cline, Joe Keaton

The Scarecrow
Script: Buster Keaton, Eddie Cline
Director: Buster Keaton, Eddie Cline
Technical director: Fred Gabourie
Photography: Elgin Lessley
Producer: Joseph M. Schenck
Production company/distributor: Comique/Metro
Cast: Buster Keaton, Joe Roberts, Sybil Seeley, Joe Keaton, Eddie Cline,
    Luke (the dog)

Neighbors
Script: Buster Keaton, Eddie Cline
Director: Buster Keaton, Eddie Cline
Technical director: Fred Gabourie
Photography: Elgin Lessley
Producer: Joseph M. Schenck
Production company/distributor: Comique/Metro
Cast: Buster Keaton, Virginia Fox, Joe Keaton, Joe Roberts, Eddie Cline,
    James Duffy

1921

The Haunted House
Script: Buster Keaton, Eddie Cline
Director: Buster Keaton, Eddie Cline
Technical director: Fred Gabourie
Photography: Elgin Lessley
Producer: Joseph M. Schenck

Production company/distributor: Comique/Metro
Cast: Buster Keaton, Virginia Fox, Joe Roberts, Eddie Cline

Hard Luck
Script: Buster Keaton, Eddie Cline
Director: Buster Keaton, Eddie Cline
Technical director: Fred Gabourie
Photography: Elgin Lessley
Producer: Joseph M. Schenck
Production company/distributor: Comique/Metro
Cast: Buster Keaton, Virginia Fox, Joe Roberts, Bull Montana

The High Sign
Script: Buster Keaton, Eddie Cline
Director: Buster Keaton, Eddie Cline
Technical director: Fred Gabourie
Photography: Elgin Lessley
Producer: Joseph M. Schenck
Production company/distributor: Comique/Metro
Cast: Buster Keaton, Al St. John, Bartine Burkett Zane

The Goat
Script: Buster Keaton, Mal St. Clair
Director: Buster Keaton, Mal St. Clair
Technical director: Fred Gabourie
Photography: Elgin Lessley
Producer: Joseph M. Schenck
Production company/distributor: Comique/Metro
Cast: Buster Keaton, Virginia Fox, Joe Roberts, Mal St. Clair, Eddie
   Cline, Jean Havez

The Boat
Script: Buster Keaton, Eddie Cline
Director: Buster Keaton, Eddie Cline
Technical director: Fred Gabourie
Photography: Elgin Lessley
Producer: Joseph M. Schenck
Production company/distributor: Comique/First National
Cast: Buster Keaton, Sybil Seeley, Eddie Cline

1922

The Paleface
Script: Buster Keaton, Eddie Cline
Director: Buster Keaton, Eddie Cline

Technical director: Fred Gabourie
Photography: Elgin Lessley
Producer: Joseph M. Schenck
Production company/distributor: Comique/First National
Cast: Buster Keaton, Joe Roberts

The Play House
Script: Buster Keaton, Eddie Cline
Director: Buster Keaton, Eddie Cline
Technical director: Fred Gabourie
Photography: Elgin Lessley
Producer: Joseph M. Schenck
Production company/distributor: Comique/First National
Cast: Buster Keaton, Joe Roberts, Virginia Fox

Cops
Script: Buster Keaton, Eddie Cline
Director: Buster Keaton, Eddie Cline
Technical director: Fred Gabourie
Photography: Elgin Lessley
Producer: Joseph M. Schenck
Production company/distributor: Comique/First National
Cast: Buster Keaton, Virginia Fox, Joe Roberts, Eddie Cline

My Wife's Relations
Script: Buster Keaton, Eddie Cline
Director: Buster Keaton, Eddie Cline
Technical director: Fred Gabourie
Photography: Elgin Lessley
Producer: Joseph M. Schenck
Production company/distributor: Comique/First National
Cast: Buster Keaton, Kate Price, Joe Roberts, Monty Collins, Wheezer
   Dell, Tom Wilson

The Blacksmith
Script: Buster Keaton, Mal St. Clair
Director: Buster Keaton, Mal St. Clair
Technical director: Fred Gabourie
Photography: Elgin Lessley
Producer: Joseph M. Schenck
Production company/distributor: Comique/First National
Cast: Buster Keaton, Virginia Fox, Joe Roberts

The Frozen North
Script: Buster Keaton, Eddie Cline
Director: Buster Keaton, Eddie Cline

Technical director: Fred Gabourie
Photography: Elgin Lessley
Producer: Joseph M. Schenck
Production company/distributor: Buster Keaton Productions/First National
Cast: Buster Keaton, Bonnie Hill, Freeman Wood, Joe Roberts, Eddie Cline

The Electric House

Script: Buster Keaton, Eddie Cline
Director: Buster Keaton, Eddie Cline
Technical director: Fred Gabourie
Photography: Elgin Lessley
Producer: Joseph M. Schenck
Production company/distributor: Buster Keaton Productions/Associated-First National
Cast: Buster Keaton, Joe Roberts, Virginia Fox, Joe, Myra, and Louise Keaton

Day Dreams

Script: Buster Keaton, Eddie Cline
Director: Buster Keaton, Eddie Cline
Technical director: Fred Gabourie
Photography: Elgin Lessley
Producer: Joseph M. Schenck
Production company/distributor: Buster Keaton Productions/Associated-First National
Cast: Buster Keaton, Renee Adoree, Joe Keaton, Joe Roberts, Eddie Cline

1923

The Balloonatic

Script: Buster Keaton, Eddie Cline
Director: Buster Keaton, Eddie Cline
Technical director: Fred Gabourie
Photography: Elgin Lessley
Producer: Joseph M. Schenck
Production company/distributor: Buster Keaton Productions/Associated-First National
Cast: Buster Keaton, Phyllis Haver

The Love Nest

Script: Buster Keaton, Eddie Cline
Director: Buster Keaton, Eddie Cline
Technical director: Fred Gabourie

Photography: Elgin Lessley
Producer: Joseph M. Schenck
Production company/distributor: Buster Keaton Productions/Associated-First National
Cast: Buster Keaton, Virginia Fox, Joe Roberts

KEATON'S SILENT FEATURES (1920–1929)

1920

The Saphead
Script: June Mathis, based on *The New Henrietta* by Winchell Smith and Victor Mapes, and *The Henrietta*, a play by Bronson Howard
Director: Herbert Blaché
Photography: Harold Wenstrom
Producer: Winchell Smith
Production company/distributor: Metro
Cast: Buster Keaton, William H. Crane, Irving Cummings, Carol Holloway, Beulah Booker, Jeffrey Williams, Edward Jobson, Edward Alexander, Jack Livingston, Edward Connelly, Odette Taylor, Katherine Albert, Helen Holte, Alfred Hollingsworth, Henry Clauss

1923

The Three Ages
Script/titles: Clyde Bruckman, Joseph Mitchell, Jean Havez
Director: Buster Keaton, Eddie Cline
Technical director: Fred Gabourie
Photography: William McGann, Elgin Lessley
Producer: Joseph M. Schenck
Production company/distributor: Metro
Cast: Buster Keaton, Margaret Leahy, Wallace Beery, Joe Roberts, Lillian Lawrence, Blanche Payson, Horace "Cupid" Morgan, Lionel Belmore

Our Hospitality
Script: Clyde Bruckman, Joseph Mitchell, Jean Havez
Director: Buster Keaton, Jack Blystone
Photography: Elgin Lessley, Gordon Jennings
Technical director: Fred Gabourie
Electrician: Denver Harmon
Costumes: Walter Israel
Producer: Joseph M. Schenck
Production company/distributor: Metro

Cast: Buster Keaton, Natalie Talmadge, Buster Keaton, Jr., Joe Keaton, Kitty Bradbury, Joe Roberts, Leonard Clapham, Craig Ward, Ralph Bushman, Edward Coxen, Jean Dumas, Monty Collins, James Duffy

1924

Sherlock Jr.
Script: Clyde Bruckman, Jean Havez, Joseph Mitchell
Director: Buster Keaton, Roscoe Arbuckle
Technical director: Fred Gabourie
Photography: Byron Houck, Elgin Lessley
Producer: Joseph M. Schenck
Production company/distributor: Metro
Cast: Buster Keaton, Kathryn McGuire, Ward Crane, Joe Keaton, Horace Morgan, Jane Connelly, Erwin Connelly, Ford West, George Davis, John Patrick, Ruth Holley

The Navigator
Script: Clyde Bruckman, Joseph Mitchell, Jean Havez
Director: Buster Keaton, Donald Crisp
Technical director: Fred Gabourie
Photography: Elgin Lessley, Byron Houck
Producer: Joseph M. Schenck
Production company/distributor: Metro-Goldwyn
Cast: Buster Keaton, Kathryn McGuire, Frederick Vroom, Clarence Burton, H. M. Clugston, Noble Johnson, Donald Crisp, Jean Havez

1925

Seven Chances
Script: Jean Havez, Clyde Bruckman, Joseph Mitchell, based on *Seven Chances,* a play by Roi Cooper Megrue
Director: Buster Keaton
Photography: Elgin Lessley, Byron Houck
Electrician: Denver Harmon
Technical director: Fred Gabourie
Producer: Joseph M. Schenck
Production company/distributor: Metro-Goldwyn
Cast: Buster Keaton, T. Roy Barnes, Snitz Edwards, Ruth Dwyer, Frankie Raymond (her mother), Jules Cowles, Erin Connelly, Jean Arthur, Loro Bara, Marion Harlan, Hazel Deane, Pauline Toler, Judy King, Eugenie Burkette, Edna Hammon, Barbara Pierce, Connie Evans, Rosalind Mooney, Jean Havez

Go West
Story: Buster Keaton
Script: Raymond Cannon
Director: Buster Keaton
Assistant director: Lex Neal
Technical director: Fred Gabourie
Photography: Elgin Lessley, Bert Haines
Producer: Joseph M. Schenck
Production company/distributor: Metro-Goldwyn
Cast: Buster Keaton, Howard Truesdale, Kathleen Myers, Ray
    Thompson, Brown Eyes, Joe Keaton, Roscoe Arbuckle, Babe London

1926

Battling Butler
Script: Paul Gerard Smith, Albert Boasberg, Lex Neal, Charles Smith,
    based on *Battling Butler*, a musical comedy by Stanley Brightman,
    Austin Melford, Philip Brabham, and Douglas Furber
Director: Buster Keaton
Photography: Dev Jennings, Bert Haines
Electrician: Ed Levy
Technical director: Fred Gabourie
Producer: Joseph M. Schenck
Production company/distributor: MGM
Cast: Buster Keaton, Sally O'Neil, Snitz Edwards, Francis McDonald,
    Mary O'Brien, Tom Wilson, Eddie Borden, Walter James, Buddy Fine

1926/7

The General
Script: Buster Keaton, Clyde Bruckman, from William Pittinger's book,
    The Great Locomotive Chase (1863)
Adaptation: Al Boasberg, Charles Smith
Director: Buster Keaton
Assistant director: Clyde Bruckman
Production manager: Fred Gabourie
Assistant production manager: H. L. Jennings
Technical director: Frank Barnes
Photography: J. Devereaux Jennings, Bert Haines, Elmer Ellsworth
Producer: Joseph M. Schenck
Production company/distributor: United Artists
Cast: Buster Keaton, Marion Mack, Glen Cavender, Jim Farley, Frederick
    Vroom, Charles Smith, Frank Barnes, Joseph Keaton, Mike Donlin,

Tom Nawn, Ray Thomas, Bud Fine, Jimmy Bryant, Red Rial, Ross McCutcheon, Red Thompson, Ray Hanford, Charles Phillips, Al Hanson, Tom Moran, Anthony Harvey, Jackie Loew, Jackie Hanlon, Jack Dempster

1927

College
Script: Carl Harbaugh, Bryan Foy
Director: James W. Home
Technical director: Fred Gabourie
Lighting: Jack Lewis
Editing: J. S. Kell
Photography: Bert Haines, Dev Jennings
Producer: Joseph M. Schenck
Supervisor: Harry Brand
Production Company/distributor: United Artist
Cast: Buster Keaton, Florence Turner, Ann Comwall, Flora Bramley, Harold Goodwin, Buddy Mason, Grant Withers, Snitz Edwards, Carl Harbaugh, Sam Crawford, Lee Barnes, Paul Goldsmith, Morton Kaer, Bud Houser, Kenneth Grumbles, Charles Borah, Leighton Dye, "Shorty" Worden, Robert Boling, Erick Mack, all of the University of Southern California baseball team

1928

Steamboat Bill Jr.
Script: Carl Harbaugh
Director: Charles F. Reisner
Assistant director: Sandy Roth
Editing: J. S. Kell
Technical director: Fred Gabourie
Photography: Dev Jermings, Bert Haines
Producer: Joseph M. Schenck
Production company/distributor: United Artists
Cast: Buster Keaton, Ernest Torrence, Tom Lewis, Tom McGuire, Marion Byron, Louise Keaton

1928

The Cameraman
Script: Clyde Bruckman, Lew Lipton
Titles: James Famham

Director: Edward M. Sedgwick
Editing: Hugh Wynn, Basil Wrangell
Technical director: Fred Gabourie
Photography: Elgin Lessley, Reggie Lanning
Producer: Buster Keaton
Production company/distributor: MGM
Cast: Buster Keaton, Marceline Day, Harold Goodwin, Harry
   Gribbon, Sidney Bracy, Edward Brophy, William Irving,
   Vernon Dent, Josephine

1929

Spite Marriage
Script: Lew Lipton, Ernest S. Pagano
Titles: Robert Hopkins
Director: Edward M. Sedgwick
Continuity: Richard Schayer
Editing: Frank Sullivan
Photography: Reggie Lanning
Producer: Edward M. Sedgwick
Supervisor: Lawrence Weingarten
Production company/distributor: MGM
Cast: Buster Keaton, Dorothy Sebastian, Edward Earle, Leila Hyams,
   William Bechtel, John Byron, Hank Mann, Pat Harmon

SOUND FEATURES STARRING KEATON (1929–1946)

1929

The Hollywood Revue of 1929
Dialogue: Al Boasberg, Robert E. Hopkins
Director: Charles Reisner
Editing: William S. Gray, Cameron K. Wood
Art director: Cedric Gibbons, Richard Day
Recording engineer: Douglas Shearer
Photography: John Amold Irving G. Ries, Maximilian Fabian, John M.
   Nickolaus
Producer: Harry Rapf
Production company/distributor: MGM
Cast: Buster Keaton, Joan Crawford, Norma Shearer, Conrad Nagel,
   John Gilbert, Laurel and Hardy, Bessie Love, Lionel Barrymore,
   Marion Davies, Marie Dressler

1930

Free and Easy
Scenario: Richard Schayer
Dialogue: Al Boasberg
Adaptation: Paul Dickey
Director: Edward M. Sedgwick
Editing: William Le Vanway, George Todd
Art director: Cedric Gibbons
Recording engineer: Douglas Shearer
Photography: Leonard Smith
Producer: Edward M. Sedgwick
Production company/distributor: MGM
Cast: Buster Keaton, Anita Page, Trixie Friganza, Robert Montgomery,
    Fred Mblo, Edgar Dearing, David Burton, Edward Brophy, Lionel
    Barrymore, Dorothy Sebastian, Jackie Coogan, Cecil B. De Mille

Doughboys
Producer: Buster Keaton
Director: Edward M. Sedgwick
Scenario: Richard Schayer
Dialogue: Al Boasberg, Richard Schayer
Story: Al Boasberg, Sidney Lazarus
Photography: Leonard Smith
Editing: William Le Vanway
Art director: Cedric Gibbons
Recording engineer: Douglas Shearer
Production company/distributor: MGM
Cast: Buster Keaton, Sally Eilers, Cliff Edwards, Edward Brophy, Victor
    Potel, Arnold Koff, Frank Mayo, Pitzy Katz, William Steele

1931

Parlor, Bedroom and Bath
Adaptation: Richard Schayer, Robert E. Hopkins, from the play by
    Charles W. Bell and Mark Swan
Director: Edward M. Sedgwick
Editing: William Le Vanway
Recording engineer: Karl Zint
Photography: Leonard Smith
Producer: Buster Keaton
Production company/distributor: MGM
Cast: Buster Keaton, Charlotte Greenway, Reginald Denny, Cliff
    Edwards, Dorothy Christy, Joan Peers, Sally Eilers, Natalie Moorhead,
    Edward Brophy, Walter Merrill, Sidney Bracy

Sidewalks of New York

Director: Jules White, Zion Meyers
Story/scenario: George Landy, Paul Gerard Smith
Dialogue: Robert E. Hopkins, Eric Hatch
Photography: Leonard Smith
Editing: Charles Hochberg
Production company/distributor: MGM
Cast: Buster Keaton, Anita Page, Cliff Edwards, Frank Rowan, Norman Phillips, Jr., Frank La Rue, Oscar Apfel, Syd Saylor, Clark Marshall

1932

The Passionate Plumber

Adaptation: Laurence E. Johnson, from *Her Cardboard Lover,* a play by Jacques Deval
Dialogue: Ralph Spence
Director: Edward M. Sedgwick
Editing: William S. Gray
Photography: Norbert Brodine
Producer: Harry Rapf
Production company/distributor: MGM
Cast: Buster Keaton, Jimmy Durante, Irene Purcell, Polly Moran, Gilbert Roland, Mona Maris, Maude Eburne, Henry Armetta, Paul Porcasi, Jean Del Val, August Tollaire, Edward Brophy

Speak Easily

Adaptation: Ralph Spence, Laurence E. Johnson, from "Footlights," a story by Clarence Budington Kelland
Director: Edward M. Sedgwick
Editing: William Le Vanway
Costumes: Arthur Appell
Photography: Harold Wenstrom
Production company/distributor: MGM
Cast: Buster Keaton, Jimmy Durante, Ruth Selwyn, Thelma Todd, Hedda Hopper, William Pawley, Sidney Toler, Lawrence Grant, Henry Armetta, Edward Brophy

1933

What, No Beer?

Script: Carey Wilson
Story: Robert E. Hopkins

Additional dialogue: Jack Cluett
Director: Edward M. Sedgwick
Editing: Frank Sullivan
Photography: Harold Wenstrom
Production company/distributor: MGM
Cast: Buster Keaton, Jimmy Durante, Roscoe Ates, Phyllis Barry, John Miljan, Henry Armetta, Edward Brophy, Charles Dunbar, Charles Giblyn

1934

Champ of the Champs Elysées
Supervisor: Robert Siodmak
Script: Arnold Lipp, Yves Mirande
Director: Max Nosseck, Bob Wyler
Art director: Hugues Laurent, Jacques-Laurent Atthalin
Music: Joe Hajos
Photography: Robert Le Febvre
Producer: Seymour Nebenzal
Production company/distributor: Nero Film Productions/Paramount (France, no U.S. release)
Cast: Buster Keaton, Paulette Dubost, Colette Darfeuil, Madeline Guitty

1936

An Old Spanish Custom
Script: Walter Greenwood
Director: Adrian Brunel
Editing: Dan Birt
Music: John Greenwood, George Rubens
Recording engineer: Scanlan
Photography: Eugene Schufftan
Producer: Sam Spiegel, Harold Richman
Production company/distributor: M. H. Hoffberg
Cast: Buster Keaton, Lupita Tovar, Esme Percy, Lyn Harding, Webster Booth, H. Maladrinos, Hilda Moreno, Clifford Heatherley

1946

Boom in the Moon
Scenario: Victor Trivas
Director: Jamie Salvador

Photography: Agustin Jiminez
Producer: Alexander Salkind
Production company/distributor: Alsa Films (Mexico; no U.S. release)
Cast: Buster Keaton, Angel Garasa, Mirginia Seret, Luis Bareiro,
   Fernando Sotto

1965

Film
Script: Samuel Beckett
Director: Alan Schneider
Editing: Sydney Myers
Photography: Boris Kaufman
Production company: Evergreen Theatre
Distributor: Grove Press
Cast: Buster Keaton

SOUND SHORT FILMS DIRECTED BY KEATON (1938)

1938

Life in Sometown, USA
Producer: Louis Lewyn
Director: Buster Keaton
Script: Carl Dudley, Richard Murphy
Production company/distributor: MGM
Narrator: Carey Wilson

Hollywood Handicap
Script: John Kraft
Director: Buster Keaton
Producer: Louis Lewyn
Production company/distributor: MGM

Streamlined Swing
Script: Marion Mack
Dialogue: John Kraft
Director: Buster Keaton
Producer: Louis Lewyn
Production company/distributor: MGM

SOUND SHORTS STARRING KEATON (1934–1941)

Allez Oop, dir. Charles Lamont (Educational, USA, 1934)

Blue Blazes, dir. Raymond Kane (Educational, USA, 1936)

Chemist, The, dir. Al Christe (Educational, USA, 1936)

Ditto, dir. Charles Lamont (Educational, USA, 1937)

E-Flat Man, The, dir. Charles Lamont (Educational, USA, 1935)

General Nuisance, Jules White (Columbia, USA, 1941)

Gold Ghost, The, dir. Charles Lamont (Educational, USA, 1934)

Grand Slam Opera, dir. Charles Lamont, scen. Keaton (Educational, USA, 1936)

Hayseed Romance, dir. Charles Lamont (Educational, USA, 1935)

His Ex Marks the Spot, Jules White (Columbia, USA, 1940)

Jail Bait, dir. Charles Lamont (Educational, USA, 1937)

Love Nest on Wheels, dir. Charles Lamont (Educational, USA, 1937)

Mixed Magic, dir. Raymond Kane (Educational, USA, 1936)

Mooching through Georgia, Jules White (Columbia, USA, 1939)

Nothing But Pleasure, Jules White (Columbia, USA, 1940)

One-Run Elmer, dir. Charles Lamont (Educational, USA, 1935)

Palooka from Paducah, dir. Charles Lamont (Educational, USA, 1935)

Pardon My Berth Marks, Jules White (Columbia, USA, 1940)

Pest from the West, Del Lord (Columbia, USA, 1939)

She's Oil Mine, Jules White (Columbia, USA, 1941)

So You Won't Squawk, Del Lord (Columbia, USA, 1941)

Spook Speaks, The, Jules White (Columbia, USA, 1940)

Taming of the Snood, The, Jules White (Columbia, USA, 1940)

Tars and Stripes, dir. Charles Lamont (Educational, USA, 1935)

Three on a Limb, dir. Charles Lamont (Educational, USA, 1936)

Timid Young Man, The, dir. Mack Sennett (Educational, USA, 1935)

ADDITIONAL FILMS CITED

Adventures of Sherlock Holmes (Vitagraph, USA, 1905)

Andalusian Dog, dir. Luis Buñuel (France, 1928)

Animal House, dir. John Landis (Universal, USA, 1977)

Annie Hall, dir. Woody Allen (United Artists, USA, 1977)

Batman Forever, dir. Joel Schumacher (Warner Bros, USA, 1995)

Beach Blanket Bingo, dir. William Asher (American-International, USA, 1965)

Benny and Joon, dir. Jeremiah S. Checkik (MGM, USA, 1993)

Bringing Up Baby, dir. Howard Hawks (RKO, USA, 1938)

Cinema Paradiso, dir. Giuseppe Tornanoya (TFI Films Production, Italy/France, 1988)

Detectress, The, dir. Gale Henry (Bullseye, USA, 1920)

Doctor Jack, dir. Fred Newmeyer (Roach/Pathé, USA, 1922)

Dumb and Dumber, dir. Peter Farrelly (New Line Cinema, USA, 1994)

From Hand to Mouth, dir. Hal Roach (Roach/Pathé, USA, 1919)

Funny Thing Happened on the Way to the Forum, A, dir. Richard Lester (United Artists, USA, 1966)

Goldfinger, dir. Guy Hamilton, (United Artists, UK, 1964)

Grandma's Boy, dir. Fred Newmeyer (Roach/Pathé, USA, 1922)

He Did and He Didn't, dir. Roscoe Arbuckle (Keystone/Triangle, USA, 1916)

His Girl Friday, dir. Howard Hawks (RKO, USA, 1940)

Intolerance, dir. D. W. Griffith (Triangle, USA, 1916)

Iron Mule, The, dir. Grover Jones (Roscoe Arbuckle) (Educational, USA, 1925)

It Happened One Night, dir. Frank Capra (Columbia, USA, 1934)

It's a Mad, Mad, Mad, Mad World, dir. Stanley Kramer (United Artists, USA, 1963)

Last Action Hero, dir. John McTierman (Columbia, USA, 1993)

Limelight, dir. Charles Chaplin (United Artists, USA, 1952)

Mask, The, dir. Chuck Russell (New Line Cinema, USA, 1994)

Mrs. Doubtfire, dir. Chris Columbus (20th Century Fox, USA, 1993)

Mystery of the Leaping Fish, The (Triangle, USA, 1916)

Palm Beach Story, The, dir. Preston Sturges (Paramount, USA, 1942)

Peter Pan, dir. Hamilton Laske (Disney, USA, 1953)

Pinocchio, dir. Ben Sharpsteen (Disney, USA, 1940)

Pretty Woman, dir. Garry Marshall (Touchstone, USA, 1990)

Purple Rose of Cairo, The, dir. Woody Allen (United Artists, USA, 1984)

Red Mill, The, dir. William Goodrich (Roscoe Arbuckle) (MGM, USA, 1927)

Round-Up, dir. George Melford (Paramount, USA, 1920)

Safety Last, dir. Fred Newmeyer, Sam Taylor (Roach/Pathé, USA, 1923)

Scandal in Bohemia, A, dir. Maurice Elvey (Alexander Film Corp., USA, 1922)

Seven Percent Solution, The, dir. Herbert Ross (Columbia, USA, 1976)

Sherlock Bonehead (USA, 1911)

Sherlock Holmes, dir. Alber Parker (Goldwin, USA, 1922)

Sherlock Holmes Baffled (Biograph, USA, 1903)

Sherlock Holmes, Junior (USA, 1911)

Something to Talk About, dir. Lasse Hallstroem (Warner Bros., USA, 1993)

Special Delivery, dir. Al St. John (Fox, USA, 1922)
Suelock Jones, Detective (USA, 1911)
Sunset Blvd., dir. Billy Wilder (Paramount, USA, 1950)
Tol'able David, dir. Henry King (First National, USA, 1921)
Trailing the Counterfeiters, dir. D.W. Griffith (Biograph, USA, 1910)
Wayne's World, dir. Penelope Spheeris (Paramount, USA, 1992)
When Harry Met Sally, dir. Rob Reiner (Columbia, USA, 1989)
Young Sherlocks, dir. Robert McGowan (Roach/Pathé, USA, 1922)

Opening Reviews of
Sherlock Jr., 1924

It is hard to imagine two more contrasting movie reviews than the *New York Times* and *Variety* pieces that follow. Keep in mind, however, that each publication has its own audience and particular focus. And for *Variety*, the industry watchdog, that focus is the box office. In fact, *Sherlock Jr.* did not make a fortune, but neither was it a complete flop, as judged in a *Motion Picture News* report.

THE NEW YORK TIMES, May 26, 1924

As one watches *Sherlock Jr.* being unfurled on the Rialto screen, one might observe with a sigh after 300 feet have passed that it is about time the comical Buster Keaton skipped into action. Just about then you realize something has happened – one of the best screen tricks ever incorporated in a comedy – and laughter starts, and for the balance of the picture you smile, snigger, chuckle, grin and guffaw.

As the embryo sleuth whose actual occupation is that of a projection machine operator in a nondescript motion picture theatre, Mr. Keaton finds the tables turned on him when the pawn ticket for a stolen watch is discovered in his own pocket. He returns to work dejected at the thought of losing his girl, and falls asleep in the operator's booth as a picture is being screened. What one sees is his dream, which in a measure is something like the dream sequence in *Hollywood.*

One views Mr. Keaton seeing his girl on the screen with the villain, he who had really stolen the watch. You see Keaton join the characters in the film he is projecting, and then he is kicked out of the picture by the villain. He is about to sit on a doorstep when the scene changes and he discovers that he is at the foot of a garden wall. The scene switches again and he narrowly escapes being run down by a train. He does get out of its way, and is then seen peering over a high cliff, which soon changes into the sight of Buster on a rock in mid ocean. He is pondering in thought, listening to the wild waves, when in comes a scene of Broadway or some traffic-congested thoroughfare. For the most part of this production our hero is endeavoring to get out of the picture he is projecting, or at least out of the swiftly changing sequences into which he has penetrated in his desire to throttle the villain, played by the sinister appearing Ward Crane.

After viewing the antics of the hero on the screen of his own theatre, the director, none other than Buster himself, has seen to it that the whole affair is brought closer so that one witnesses the full size result. Of course the first part of this long sequence is boisterously funny, and nary the flicker of expression crosses the Keaton countenance, except through the eyes. His face might be made of stone for all the resiliency there is in it.

This is an extremely good comedy which will give you plenty of amusement so long as you permit Mr. Keaton to glide into his work with his usual deliberation.

[*Editor's note:* It is interesting how plain wrong the piece is on details even though the reviewer clearly adopts a thumbs-up attitude. The rendering of the plot is quite awkward and misleading: why not do as the film does and say the Keaton figure has two interests, winning the girl and being a detective? And Keaton is not trying to get out of the film once he is "on screen"; he is trying to solve the crime and win the girl!]

━━━━━━━━━

VARIETY, May 28, 1924

This Buster Keaton feature length comedy is about as unfunny as a hospital operating room. It is far and away about the most laughter lacking picture that "Dead Pan" Buster has turned out in a long long while. The running time of the picture is such that it is far better suited to run at the finish of a program in which there is a good strong feature. That is about the only way that this picture will turn any money back to the exhibitors who play it. Although it is on Broadway this week in a pre-release house, the Rialto, [there] is no reason that the average exhibitor has to believe that it is worthy of having that honor. In other words, it's a flop, and the week's box office receipts at the Rialto will undoubtedly prove that to be the case.

The picture has about all the old hoke that there is in the world in it. That ranges from a piece of business with a piece of flypaper to a money changing bit, and, for added good measure, a chase. There are, in fact, two chases: that means another one was thrown in for good measure, but neither of these chases can for a single second hold a candle to the chase that Harold Lloyd staged in his last picture [*Girl Shy*, 1924] and in comparison they appear as child's play.

There is one piece of business, however, that is well worked out and that is worthy of comment. It is the bit where Buster as a motion picture machine operator in a dream scene walks out of the booth and into the action that is taking place on the screen of the picture that he is projecting. That is clever. The rest is bunk.

The chances are that this picture will turn about the lowest gross of any of the Keatons that Metro has thus far handled.

━━━━━━━━━

MOTION PICTURE NEWS, May 3, 1924
(Vol. 29, No. 18), p. 1995

Newspaper and public were agreed that it is one of the best Keaton has yet turned out, with many new and clever stunts. Brought the laughs all right. Business fair.

MOTION PICTURE NEWS, May 17, 1924 (Vol. 29, No. 20), p. 2365

Isn't a dull moment. . . . Constant humor all the way. . . . Clever satire.

Laurence Reid

PHOTOPLAY, July 1924 (Vol. 26), p. 46

Buster Keaton with a lot of new gags. He appears as a young man with a flair for amateur sleuthing. He has radical adventures. This is by no means Keaton's most hilarious offering, but it is short, snappy and amusing. Comedies are like oases in a celluloid world, rare and refreshing, and you don't want to miss Buster with his immobile face and unique composure in his new setting.

Select Bibliography

ON COMEDY AND FILM COMEDY

No effort is made to be more than suggestive here since "film comedy" embraces sound comedy in all its forms, which is not the focus of this volume. These works, however, cover issues and topics beyond more narrowly focused "sound" comedies such as the screwball romantic comedy.

Calhoon, Kenneth S. "The Detective and the Witch: Local Knowledge in Conan Doyle and Fontane." Forthcoming in *Comparative Literature* 47:4 (1995): 307–29.

Durgnat, Raymond. *The Crazy Mirror: Hollywood Comedy and the American Image*. London: Faber & Faber, 1969.

Eco, Umberto, and Thomas A. Sebeok. *The Sign of Three: Dupin, Holmes, Peirce*. Bloomington: Indiana University Press, 1983.

Frye, Northrop. *Anatomy of Criticism: Four Essays*. Princeton, NJ: Princeton University Press, 1957.

Girard, René. *Deceit, Desire and the Novel*. Baltimore: Johns Hopkins Press, 1965.

Haskell, Molly. *From Reverence to Rape*. New York: Holt, Rinehart & Winston, 1974.

Isherwood, Christopher. " 'The Speckled Band' by Arthur Conan Doyle." In *Exhumations*. Harmondsworth: Penguin, 1969, pp. 55–70.

Karnick, Kristine Brunovska, and Henry Jenkins. *Classical Hollywood Comedy*. New York: Routledge, Chaplin & Hall, 1995.

Kracauer, Sigfried. *From Caligari to Hitler*. Princeton, NJ: Princeton University Press, 1947.

Horton, Andrew (ed.). *Comedy/Cinema/Theory*. Berkeley: University of California Press, 1991.

Jenkins, Henry. *What Made Pistachio Nuts? Early Sound Comedy and the Vaudeville Aesthetic*. New York: Columbia University Press, 1992.

Kundera, Milan. *The Art of the Novel*. Translated by Linda Asher. New York: Grove Press, 1988.

Lahue, Kalton, and Samuel Gill. *Clown Princes and Court Jesters*. New York: Barnes, 1970.

Marcus, Steven. *Freud and the Culture of Psychoanalysis*. London: George Allen & Unwin, 1984.

Mast, Gerald. *The Comic Mind: Comedy and the Movies*. New York: Bobbs-Merrill, 1973, esp. chap. 9 on Keaton, pp. 125–46.

Modleski, Tania. *Studies in Entertainment*. Bloomington: Indiana University Press, 1986.

Montgomery, John. *Comedy Films, 1894–1954*. London: George Allen & Unwin, 1954; revised 1968.

Neale, Steve, and Frank Krutnik. *Popular Film and Television Comedy*. London: Routledge, 1990.

Palmer, Jerry. *Logic of the Absurd*. London: British Film Institute, 1987.

Rowe, Kathleen. *The Unruly Woman: Gender and the Genres of Laughter*. Austin: University of Texas Press, 1995.

Seidman, Steve. *Comedian Comedy: A Tradition in Hollywood Film*. Ann Arbor, MI: UMI Research, 1981.

ON SILENT COMEDY

Brownlow, Kevin. *The Parade's Gone By*. . . . New York: Knopf, 1968.

Brownlow, Kevin, and David Gill. "Harold Lloyd: The Third Genius." PBS, 1989.

"The Unknown Chaplin." PBS, 1985.

Dardis, Tom. *Harold Lloyd: The Man on the Clock*. New York: Viking Press, 1983.

Edmonds, Andy. *Frame Up: The Untold Story of Roscoe "Fatty" Arbuckle*. New York: Morrow, 1991.

Kerr, Walter. *The Silent Clowns*. New York: Knopf, 1975.

Lahue, Kalton C. *World of Laughter: The Motion Picture Comedy Short, 1910–1930*. Norman: University of Oklahoma Press, 1966.

MacCann, Richard Dyer (ed.). *The Silent Comedians*. Metuchen, NJ: Scarecrow Press, 1993.

Robinson, David. *Chaplin: His Life and Art*. New York: McGraw-Hill, 1985.

Yallop, David A. *The Day the Laughter Stopped: The True Story of Fatty Arbuckle*. New York: St. Martin's Press, 1976.

BY KEATON

Keaton, Buster, with Charles Samuels. *My Wonderful World of Slapstick*. New York: Doubleday, 1960.

"Why I Never Smile." *Ladies' Home Journal* 43:6 (June 26, 1926): 20, 173–4.

ON KEATON

For the definitive word on Keaton scholarship we recommend consulting Joanna Rapf and Gary L. Green's recent book listed below. Readers are alerted that there is an International Buster Keaton Society, The Damfinos, with its own newsletter. Those interested should contact The Damfinos, c/o Melody Bunting, 161 West 75th St., Apt 14F, New York, NY 10023; phone: 212/799-4949; fax: 212/580-8698; e-mail: jpkm44@ prodigy.com.

New web sites seem to spring up almost weekly, but as this book goes to print, here are the most important Keaton-related sites: Australia: http://www.noa.gov.au/2/film/keaton.mtml; Canada: http://www. net. bistro.com./buster/htm; Germany: http://www.informatik.unifreiburt. de\~aka\ws95\buster.html; Great Britain: Buzzard@dial.pipex.com; United States (the New York–based Silent Majority Page, which wants to get all silent movie stars covered on the Web): http:// www.dle. om/classicfilms/featuredstar/star3.htm.

Roscoe "Fatty" Arbuckle, Keaton's mentor, exists at a web site established by David Pearson of this volume: http://www.uno.edu/drif/ arbuckle.

Agee, James. "Great Stone Face." *Life* 27 (September 5, 1949): 84–5.

Benayoun, Robert. "Le colosse de silence." *Positif*, nos. 77–8 (Summer 1966): 18–24. (A study of Keaton and Franz Kafka, with Keaton about to triumph over adverse situations.)
The Look of Buster Keaton. Edited and translated by Randall Conrad. New York: St. Martin's Press, 1983 (Paris, 1982).

Bishop, Christopher. "The Great Stone Face." *Film Quarterly* 12:1 (Fall 1958): 10–15.

"An Interview with Buster Keaton," *Film Quarterly* 12:1 (Fall 1958): 15–22.

Blesh, Rudi. *Keaton*. New York: Collier Books, 1966.

Brownlow, Kevin, and David Gill. *Buster Keaton: A Hard Act to Follow*. Part One: "From Vaudeville to Movies"; Part Two: "Star Without a Studio"; Part Three: "A Genius Recognized." (A three-set video tape collection made by Thames Television PLC, 1987. Fifty-two minutes each, with many clips from the films and narration by Lindsay Anderson. Made in association with Raymond Rohauer.)

Carroll, Noël, "Notes on the Sight Gag." In *Comedy/Film/Theory*. Edited by Andrew Horton. Berkeley: University of California Press, 1991, pp. 25–42.

"Buster Keaton: Film Acting as Action." In *Making Visible the Invisible*. Edited by C. Zucker. Metuchen, NJ: Scarecrow Press, 1990, pp. 198–223.

Cecchi, Alberto. "Nota su Buster Keaton." *La Fiera Letteraria*, December 29, 1929, p. 15.

Coursodon, Jean-Pierre. *Buster Keaton*. Paris: Seghers, 1973.

Dardis, Tom. *Keaton: The Man Who Wouldn't Lie Down*. New York: Limelight Editions, 1988.

Demun, Philipe, et al. "Buster est de retour." *Contre-Champ*, no. 3 (May 1962). (Whole issue devoted to Keaton.)

Gillett, John, and James Blue. "Keaton at Venice." *Sight and Sound* 35:1 (Winter 1965): 26–30. (An interview.)

Gilliatt, Penelope. "Buster Keaton." In *Unholy Fools: Wits, Comics, Disturbers of the Peace: Film & Theatre*. New York: Viking Press, pp. 45–54.

Herman, Hal C. (ed.). *How I Broke into Movies: Signed Autobiographies by Sixty Famous Stars*. Hollywood: Hal C. Herman, 1928.

Kline, Jim. *The Complete Films of Buster Keaton*. New York: Citadel Press, 1993.

Kramer, Peter. "The Making of a Comic Star: Buster Keaton and *The Saphead*." In *Classical Hollywood Comedy*. Edited by Kristine Brunovska Karnick and Henry Jenkins. Routledge, Chaplin & Hall. New York, 1995, pp. 190–210.

Lebel, Jean-Pierre. *Buster Keaton*. Paris: Editions universitaires, 1964. Translated from the French by P. D. Stavin. New York: Barnes, 1967.

McCaffrey, Donald W. "The Mutual Approval of Keaton and Lloyd." *Cinema Journal* 6 (1966–7): 9–15.

Moews, Daniel. *Keaton: The Silent Features Close Up*. Berkeley: University of California Press, 1977.

Parshall, Peter F. "Buster Keaton and the Space of Farce: *Steamboat Bill*,

Jr. versus *The Cameraman.*" *Journal of Film and Video* 46:3 (Fall 1944): 29–46.

Rapf, Joanna, and Gary L. Green. *Buster Keaton: A Bio-Bibliography.* Westport, CT: Greenwood Press, 1995.

"Buster Keaton and Jimmy Durante: Mesh, Match, or Blend!" Paper delivered at the Society for Cinema Studies Conference, New York, March 1995.

Robinson, David. *Buster Keaton.* 2d ed. London: Secker & Warburg, 1970.

Sanders, Judith, and Daniel Liberfeld. "Dreaming in Pictures: The Childhood Origins of Buster Keaton's Creativity." *Film Quarterly* 47:4 (Summer 1994): 14–28.

Sweeny, Kevin W. "Parody and Comic Revision in Keaton's Features." Paper delivered at the Society for Cinema Studies Conference, New York, March 1995.

Wead, George, and George Lellis. *The Film Career of Buster Keaton.* Pleasantville, NY: Redgrave, 1977.

Wolfe, Charles. "Keaton and Historical Fiction." Paper delivered at the Society for Cinema Studies Conference, New York, March 1995.

ON *SHERLOCK JR.*

Clair, René. *Reflexion faite.* Paris: Editions Gallimard, pp. 107, 225. (The surrealism of the film.)

Laura, Ernesto G. "Buster Keaton nel periodo muto." *Bianco e Nero* 24:9–10 (September–October 1963): 82–107. (Levels of satire of American life and cinema itself in this film.)

Mannes, George. " 'Jr.' Achievement." *Entertainment Weekly,* January 21, 1994, p. 55.

Rodowick, David. *"Sherlock Jr.* Program Notes." *Cinema Texas* (University of Texas, Austin), March 3, 1977.

Trahair, Lisa. "Fool's Gold: The Metamorphosis of Buster Keaton's *Sherlock, Jr.*" Paper delivered at the Society for Cinema Studies Conference, New York, March 1995.

Index